SHOW ME A FIREFIGHTER

By
Josh Shroyer

WORDS MATTER
PUBLISHING
OUR WORDS CHANGE THE WORLD

Words Matter Publishing
P.O. Box 1190
Decatur, IL 62525
www.wordsmatterpublishing.com

ISBN 13: 978-1-962467-97-1

Library of Congress Catalog Card Number: 2025941524

Dedication

This book is dedicated to Nate and Drew,
who insisted I write these stories down.

Acknowledgments

I would like to acknowledge all the friends and mentors not only from my career, but from my life, who have been a part of this wonderful journey. A special acknowledgement to those who so graciously allowed me to use their photos of me to help tell this story, and especially Kari Greer and Kristen Honig, whose professional photography was so top-notch. To friend and mentor Tim Stanton, who pushed through to publish his book, which helped me break through some mental and emotional barriers so I could finish my book. To Words Matter Publishing, who have been so great and easy to work with. To my family for all the support. To Nate, who kept asking to hear these stories over and over, and most importantly, to my wife, Tammy, who has stuck by my side through all the good and bad of this crazy career that has given me these stories.

Table of Contents

Prologue

This book is a collection of memories and perspectives I have gained over the years of working wildfires. Some are short stories; some are a little longer. Some have a bit of humor in them, while others may be a little bit serious. Almost all have some lessons that can be learned if you dig deep enough, while some I hopefully have made the lesson to be learned come out and slap you in the face. They are my stories, my memories, my perceptions of what happened. I may have changed some of the names to protect both the guilty and the innocent and out of respect for private moments. A lot of these stories have been told to my kids about a thousand times, as they always wanted to hear them. Of course, this is how some of the more humorous stories have come about. I feel it is best when you can laugh at yourself, as anyone who can't is taking life much too seriously. I also believe that truth is stranger and, many times, funnier than fiction. You just can't make this stuff up. I mean, can you imagine what it feels like to have your pants down knowing there is a mountain lion close? Keep reading, and you may find out.

Throughout my career, I have met many fine firefighters. I have also met some that I really wonder how they passed their basic fire training. As I consider myself a student of fire, I am always trying to learn something new from those guys who have been around for a while. Everyone has different experiences and perspectives, and I love swapping stories, as that is where some of the best tidbits of knowledge get passed around. On this note, I guess that is part of the reason for writing this book. Maybe I can pass on some tidbits of knowledge and information to another firefighter or at least relate some funny story that they can use to relieve some stress. I remember a conversation I had with a fellow fire trainer; he said that we all have an obligation to pass on what we have learned to the newer firefighters so that maybe we can keep someone safe someday.

There are stories that relay things that we don't do anymore. Some of this is that times change, technology gets better, or our society has gotten softer and more prone to being offended, I don't know. I guess I don't really care. What happened in the past happened, and it made for some good memories and stories. Some things I am glad have changed. Some things I wish would not have changed.

For this book, I have decided to keep mostly good times and fond memories. Yes, there are many dark, sad, and tragic stories, but that may be for a different time and different place. I once heard another firefighter put it something like this, we try to concentrate on the good and suppress the bad. I think that is wonderful advice. With that said, some of these are "fond memories." Many great firefighters I have worked with through the years and learned from have already passed on to a better place. I do wish I could visit with them again, as there are always more questions to ask, but I will cherish the memories I had with them, even if it does mean a little bit of dust gets blown into my eye on occasion.

As for the title, Show Me a Firefighter, I am from Missouri, "The Show Me State." This nickname for Missouri that refers to the state's reputation for skepticism, and need for proof. The phrase is often used to describe someone who is unwilling to accept something without evidence. Well, I resemble that remark most days, as I have always had a bit of skepticism in matters that really matter. Now, to the name play, I want to Show You the perspectives of a wildland firefighter from Missouri. Though I am now located in Wyoming and have traveled most of the western two-thirds of the country, my roots run deep.

So, with that, please sit back and enjoy this collection. Hopefully, you will laugh a bit and also think back to some of your stories and memories. I think we all have more in common than we realize, no matter where we are from or where we fight fires.

Chapter 1

Where I Come From

What Makes Me, well, Me?

This first chapter is to give a brief history and background, as well as define some of the terms I use in later chapters. Um, on second thought, terms can be their own chapter. I guess you will have to read that one when you get to it.

I have always been called to the outdoors. I grew up in the river hills next to the bottoms of the Mighty Missouri River. I am firmly in the middle of the Gen X generation, where I was a Latch-Key Kid during school and a "be home before nightfall" kind of summer. No, my parents still don't realize how far I rode my bike some days. So much of my early life was about learning to survive and becoming self-sufficient. By the age of 12, I knew what I wanted to do and be, thanks a lot to my uncle being a forester and wildland firefighter. I did the scouting thing and campouts and earned my Eagle Scout at 13 years and 2 months old. I hunted, fished, and trapped. We lived on a steep hill in town, and I learned to drive a stick on that hill.

I could write an entire book on my childhood, but maybe I'll save that for another day. I think I'll just give you enough here to paint the picture of where I come from.

I had a lot of influences early on. My love for baseball came from my dad and my maternal grandmother and translated into a short stint of junior college ball before a shoulder injury sidetracked that dream. Forward a couple of years, I was going to try to walk on for the University of Missouri ball team, but I decided that I truly wanted to chase two other things. First, and most importantly, my soon-to-be wife and my dream of being a forester and firefighter.

Both of my parents were school teachers, and I learned about the importance of studying, not only in books but by observing the world around me. I also learned that I couldn't get away with as much as my other Gen X counterparts, as it seemed that teachers always found out things, and when your parents are also teachers, well, you know.

My grandpa, Jack, who only had up to an 8th-grade education, was probably the smartest man I have ever known. He worked hard and had an engineer's mind. He could figure out the mechanics of anything and was a top-notch woodworker and builder. I also learned to never stop learning. At the age of 78 or 80, this man, with only an 8th-grade education, borrowed a couple of books from the library and taught himself calculus! I struggled to barely pass calculus in college. I hated that class. He learned it just to challenge himself and learn something new.

From my uncle, I learned the finer details of hunting and fishing and listened to his exploits of fighting wildfires and working in the trees. This cemented my desire to become a forester myself, fight the fires, and "live among the trees."

A handful of slightly older guys from around the community took it upon themselves to help teach me how to be a trapper. Scott, Ed, Curtis, and Brian somehow took me in and got me started and willingly shared their secrets for a good mink or muskrat set, where to scout for beaver signs, or how to listen to the howls of the coon dogs. This trapping career lasted my entire high school years, and many nights, I was running my trap line in the dark after getting home from a late basketball practice or game. This was a line that ran from right near the house up a drainage ditch and back on the other side. Looking now, it was 1.3 miles one way and 2.6 miles round trip, before I could legally drive. In the dark, by myself, hauling everything I needed, and caught. One night, I trapped two beavers over the 40-pound mark, which made for a tough walk back after a particularly grueling practice. After I got my driver's license, I expanded my lines and could get farther from home.

Back to Brian, my cousin. Well, I guess second cousin. My mom's cousin, to be exact. He was the closest thing I had to a big brother. I credit him for many things. He kept me going in scouts, even after I earned my Eagle Scout. Most boys quit once they achieved that, but he kept me involved and encouraged. He taught me how to skin muskrats and coons, and how to prepare the hides for sale. He showed me his trapping methods and let me tag along on his trap line early on. He was my introduction to the fire service. His dad was a long-time fire chief in town, and Brian followed and, at the time, soon became the Assistant Fire Chief. I remember one house fire we were fighting together. I was on the nozzle, and he was right behind me. We made entry and were working down the hall to find the fire. We found it in a room, and due to a miscommunication with the outside crews, the wrong window was broken out for ventilation. When we opened up on the fire, there was nowhere for it to go, and it flashed over the top of us. Brian kept his composure and backed us out as fast as we could to the entry point, where we started over. We ended up getting that knocked down fairly quickly, but I knew then, as I had learned many times before, Brian was one I needed to keep learning from, and he was always watching out for me.

I was a "town kid." I can't say city kid, as our town was only 700 people at the time, but I had many friends who were farm kids, so I had the benefit of learning farm life. We walked beans, cut and hoed weeds, we were on hay crews where we picked up and stacked square bales, worked cattle, I learned how to drive a tractor, and learned how to think outside the box to fix something when it was broken. These farm kids could always (and probably still to this day) outwork me. That is the nature of farm kids.

I never knew how poor we really were while I was growing up. My parents worked odd jobs outside of teaching, so we always had food on the table. But through some of these odd jobs, I learned other skills. My mom would take on extra duties, such as the drama coach, where I learned how to act in school plays and write articles for the school yearbook, as she was the Yearbook Coordinator. I learned how to roof by working with Dad on roofing jobs during the summer, working on concrete, framing a house, or building cabinets, or, well, you get the picture. I had my first "business" before I was a teenager mowing yards and had a contract with the church to mow the church lawn and cemetery. Later, I had a firewood business where I would cut, split, and deliver firewood.

In college, I think I spent every spring break on a job or making money somehow. I never did the typical college spring break party animal thing. I would help with wildfires in the Ozarks of Missouri or some of us forestry students would bid on and work on Forest Service slashing contracts, where we would go into an area that had a previous timber sale and slash down the rest of the trees so the regeneration could take off. I even had a job in the dungeon, or I mean basement, of the Ag Building at Mizzou cleaning, cracking, separating, and weighing walnuts for some research project. Talk about cramped hands and bleeding raw fingers. All for $3.75 per hour.

I believe all of this so far prepared me for what I was to do later in life. Working alone in the dark after a fire had been put out was no big deal as I had been alone on those trap lines long before. Being able to fix a piece of equipment that broke down on a fire was no big deal, as I learned that early on as well. I rather enjoyed the alone parts of the job. Although some of that that and the job has changed over the years, I still am perfectly at home in the woods by myself or on a lonely section of the fire line. Some great stories come from being alone, as you will read. Others can only be good stories because of the company I had.

I will never admit to being perfect. I was, and am still, far from it. I used to have a rather foul mouth at times and maybe have done some questionable things in the past. However, I have worked hard to clean up my language. Some of the stories, if there is an inserted dialog, have the cleaned-up version, but if something slips in, I apologize. I firmly believe you can tell a great story without being foul-mouthed. In fact, as I advanced in my fire career, it just seemed unprofessional to say some words, no matter what the situation was. Those who speak to the public or where the public can hear represent the larger fire service profession, and we owe it to them to be the better person.

As I mentioned in the prologue, this concentrates on the good stories, but please understand the bad stories are just as much a part of me; I just choose to not share them here. I believe that the kindest people in the world have had some of the darkest stories. They just choose to keep those hidden and project goodness, partially due to the fact that they know what the darkness is and don't want anyone else to have to suffer that.

Laugh at life; laugh at yourself. Treat others the way you want to be treated. Be the bigger person, but don't allow yourself to get walked over, either. Smile often and share that smile with others. Hold the door for a stranger. Lend a comforting ear without judgment. Learn to show emotion. Love everyone, but especially love yourself. Take care of yourself so that you can take care of your neighbor. This is where I come from.

Photo of cousin Brian and I at my Eagle Scout Court of Honor.
I think I had my Forrest Gump vibe going that day.
Photo by: Shroyer Family Archives

Photo of my family. Mom, Kathy, me, my youngest brother
Jordan being held by my dad, Chuck, and my younger brother, Thomas.
Photo by: Shroyer Family Archives

Chapter 2

Fire Towers

My Time Above the Forest

I feel a connection with fire towers. I guess I like the connection to the older technology. A simpler time. A simpler place.

I had the good fortune to sit in a number of towers early on in my career. I got to meet some really interesting old Towermen/Firefighters. This was at a time when towers were going out of style, and newer technology was coming up. We started using planes for aerial detection more, and once cell phones came around, the concerned public could overload a dispatch office with reports of a fire. I consider myself lucky to have gotten in on the tail end of the Fire Tower era in Missouri.

I had no formal training on towers or the fire finders in them. I learned everything from impromptu sessions with the older Towermen.

On my first tower assignment, I met up with an old, battle-weary District Forester named Noble. He was very short and simple in his instructions.

"There's the tower," he said. "Head on up and meet with the guy up there."

That was it. Nothing more. No explanation of what to do once I got up there, or what I might expect to learn. Just—head up the steps.

The tower was pretty standard for Missouri towers—100 feet tall, with a 7-foot by 7-foot cabin on top. Inside, a single stool and an Osborne Fire Finder.

As I climbed the steel tower, I had no idea what—or who—to expect when I got to the cabin. Did he even know I was coming?

As I reached the cabin, I knocked on the "door" at the top of the steps, and it opened. Standing there, looking down at me, was a very grizzled-looking firefighter in a dirty yellow shirt, stained with the smoke and soot of many fires.

He opened with, "It took you long enough to climb those stairs. Come on in."

Great. I had failed my first test. I took too long to climb the 100 feet of steps.

As I stepped into the cabin, I immediately noticed how cramped it was. The fire finder was located in the center of the room, and there was enough room to walk completely around the table. He had some windows open, and the cool breeze was blowing in. He introduced himself as Mark. We exchanged a quick introduction of each other and why I was there. Mark turned out to be very friendly and had a very dry sense of humor. I think he understood my interest and offered up a lot of information.

He showed me how to use the fire finder. Where to stand in the tower to get the best views of the problem fire areas. He showed me how to read smoke out in the hills and on the horizon. He went over the radio procedure for calling in a potential fire and pointed out directions to other fire towers in the district.

He had me practice on a number of smokes already standing up. I would "find" the fire on the finder and jot down the info as if I were going to call it in. Then he would tell me what was going on with that smoke. One was an actual fire that others were already fighting. One was a controlled burn, or prescribed fire, in a State Park. Another was a smoke plume from a charcoal plant, and so on. As the afternoon wore on, we called in a couple of new smokes, and the Dispatcher triangulated from other towers and sent out firefighters to fight them. Finally, a good smoke rose up that seemed closer and possibly in our area. I got to "find" it, but he called it in on the radio. Sure enough, it was in our area, and all the other firefighters were out on other fires, so we were sent to fight it. We gathered our stuff and started down the steps.

I rode with Mark to the fire. I asked who would be coming to help us, and he just chuckled. It was just going to be us. We got to the fire and met up with the landowner. This was a controlled burn that got out of hand. The good thing for us was that there were a number of trails through the woods that we could utilize to help contain this fire. Between our leaf blowers, leaf rakes, and a drip torch, we were able to use and connect trails to finally contain the fire at about 40 acres. We mopped up a little, left the fire with the landowner, and headed back to our tower. A Towerman's job is never done.

Just as we were pulling into the parking lot for our tower, we got called to another fire. This one, we were going to help some other firefighters who were already working it. This second fire went quicker than the first, and it was dark when we got back to the tower. We had already been notified that we were probably going to yet another fire, but Dispatch wanted another tower to shoot an azimuth and give a bearing, as they were having a hard time triangulating it. We climbed the tower in the dark, more by feel, since we didn't want to lose our night vision.

When we reached the cabin, Mark brought out a red headlamp so we could safely get in, and then we scanned the horizon for the glow of the fire. Finally, we found it and used the red light to get our reading for Dispatch. Then we headed back down to the truck. When we got to the fire, we were not the first ones there. A number of other district guys were there as they had also finished up their other fires from earlier in the day. This fire was stretched out over many hollers and ridges. We worked on this fire until the early hours of the morning. I think I got back about 4am that morning. When Mark dropped me off at my truck, he said to meet him back at the tower at 10am, and we would do it all over again. So ended my first day as a Towerman. Three ascents of the tower, three fires worked, five fires called in, and an 18-hour day.

I would go on to spend a number of days in that tower with Mark, and we struck up a good friendship that would last for many years. We fought many fires together and had many stories to swap. Years later, through a series of events, we ended up working together again. This time, I was in the neighboring district, and we were now part of the West Central Region. While we each worked in our own areas, the finicky nature of fires in our area allowed us to work fires together from time to time. Most of the time, when a fire was done, we ended up recalling some long-lost day spent in the tower or some late-night fire just he and I worked together. Our friendship lasted for the rest of his life, and as with the loss of any good friend, it was bittersweet to attend his memorial at that very tower, where a memorial stone was placed to honor his many years of dedication. It was, and always will be, Mark's Tower to me.

While I got to sit in other towers during my career, the days were limited. As I said, the plane was making towers obsolete. Additionally, there were more and more people getting mobile phones. It started with bag phones mainly, but as technology got better, more people got cell phones, and fire towers were used less and less. Some days, when I was flying fire patrol in one of our Agency planes, we would fly over an old tower. The pilot and I would talk about days gone by, but the discussion would be interrupted by the sight of yet another smoke to check out.

It has now been many years since I spotted a smoke from a tower and used the Osborne Fire Finder. I still love fire towers. As I travel this great country of ours, I am always on the lookout for a tower. Once, when my family was on vacation, we drove through the planted Nebraska National Forest, and I had to stop by and climb the fire tower that was put up to protect that forest. Another time, I was on a fire detail in Washington and ended up with a day free to sightsee before my flight home. I looked at the map and noticed a fire tower close by. Guess where I spent half a day exploring? You got that right. I drove up the winding road and visited Leecher Lookout. This is a newer tower at about 40 feet to the cabin. I enjoyed the views from this tower, but I had read about the original lookout tree just down the ridge and had to go exploring to find it. Some of the original lookouts were just trees that they climbed, cut the top out, and built a small cabin on. I finally found it and took a photo from the base of the tree, looking straight up along the old moss-covered wooden ladder rails. I didn't think much more about that photo until I got home and my wife was looking through my pictures. She liked it so much that we enlarged it and framed it, and it now graces a wall in our house.

It pains me to see a lot of old fire towers disappearing from the horizon. I fully understand that it is hard to maintain something that is not used anymore. But still, I just cringed when we sold an old, outdated tower for one dollar, which was just going to be torn down and sold for scrap. The stories that could be told from those cabins, looking down on the canopy of trees, would fill volumes. I wish I could have bought one myself and restored it to its original grandeur. Alas, without a large crane, I would not have been able to complete the removal contract in time.

Whether you have never been up a fire tower, or it has been a long time, or even if you just were up one recently, I think everyone should experience the thrill of the view from a fire tower, looking over the forest that it was designed to watch over. This brings me to my final thoughts on fire towers. If you can take a loved one to a fire tower, you really need to. I had a chance early on to show my young wife the romantic side of fire towers. This was before we had children, and I was on a temporary duty assignment to the deep Ozarks. I convinced my wife to come down and spend a weekend with me as I was staying in an old Towerman's House on Coot Mountain. This was a tower that was not in much use, and the Agency no longer housed a full-time towerman at the location, so the house sat vacant, except for use by employees on special assignments like I was. She came down, and, after cooking a quick meal, we climbed the Coot Mountain Fire Tower to just below the cabin, about 60 feet, short for Missouri tower standards. We just sat on one of the steps and watched the beautiful sunset over the Ozark hills. What a view. What a memory. A simpler time. A simpler place.

Photo of the Camdenton Fire Tower. This is the first tower I was ever in and where I met Mark.

A view from just under the cabin of the Camdenton
Fire Tower looking out over the Ozark Hills.

A selfie I took while on a fire assignment in New Mexico. During our Liaison
travels we stopped at the Bandolier National Monument and I was able to
visit the Bandolier Lookout, complete with Osborne Fire Finder.

Photo of Leecher Lookout in Washington.

Photo I took of the original lookout tree on Leecher Mountain.

Photo of the Coot Mountain Fire Tower.

Chapter 3

Early Lesson

Can you spare a second or two?

At this point, I was a brand-new supervisor at a new work location. We got called to a small wildfire in the oak-hickory leaf litter, and it was just my Forest Technician and me responding late this evening. Since I was new to the area, I took the lead from my Tech, an older employee who had 20 years of experience in this area fighting fires. I was young and gung-ho and wanted to show that I was cut out for this, so I got right to work using the leaf rake to "dig" a line, clearing the leaves down to bare soil to create the fire line. I was head-down, staying just far enough away from the fire to not be too hot, as we were on the flank of the fire.

I noticed my Tech kind of staying back and burning out the lines. This is a normal tactic, especially with only 2 of us on this fire. We could stay together in case either needed help. However, it seemed like he had a smirk on his face, but I dismissed it. Maybe he was just watching this new guy with all this energy and allowing me to do all the work. Anyway, I finally got around the small fire, maybe 3-4 acres or so, and we started cleaning up the edges a bit better. I was hot and tired, and it was late in the day by this time, and my Tech finally chuckled a bit. I couldn't stand it anymore, so I asked what was going on. He calmly said to follow him.

As we made our way back to the road where I had started my rake line, he stopped. Finally, he asked me to look around. What did I see? Did I even see anything? I didn't know what he was getting at. I had made a great rake line. It held perfectly, and the fire was out. What was the problem? Then, he proceeded to show me that no more than 20 yards from my rake line was a small creek with running water. I had run parallel to this creek for a long way before I "turned" the corner. Yup, I finally realized my mistake. Had I just used the small creek as a natural fire break, I would have saved myself a ton of work that night. I could have just walked to the far end of the fire, tied into the creek, and started up the hill, and not only saved all that work, but I would have been done a lot sooner as well, maybe even half the time, or less.

The lesson was to not get tunnel vision and keep your head up and see the whole picture. I was so focused on making a good impression that I missed an easy way to fight this fire. Since that day, I have always taken a few extra seconds and looked around at the whole picture, my whole surrounding, before engaging the fire. Lessons like this are best taught by learning the hard way. Had he tried to tell me, I may have bucked him as I was too focused. But by expending all that energy, mentally, I was able to accept the lesson. I have used this technique on many new employees since then. When it is safe to do so, I allow room to fail or work the long way around. Each time, those who made the "mistake" are always ready to accept the lesson. You can always spare a second or two to evaluate before you engage. Thankfully, he never really brought this lesson-learning incident up. Well, not too much, anyway.

Even though I "supervised" Chipper, he did more to supervise
and mentor me, especially in those first few months. Sometimes,
his look alone could speak volumes without ever saying a word.

Although from later in my career, I took a minute to
just appreciate this view.

Chapter 4

Dynamite Got Run Over
by a White Tail

Don't Forget the Catchy Tune

It was mid-April, and the fire season had been fairly slow. We had had some well-timed moisture all of March and the first weeks of April, and the grass was getting pretty green. Live fuel moistures in the cedar were also fairly high, so many fires we had were fairly low intensity but very smoky.

We got the call just after lunch, a possible arson fire in some overgrown old field. There was a lot of cedar in the area with wide crowns that went all the way to the ground. You could walk between the trees, but it was like walking through a maze. I had about an hour's drive from my office to get to the fire, so the rest of my crew was there before I was. I established radio contact when I arrived on the scene and found out where to meet up with the rest of the crew. We found each other and talked about the plans for the fire. Chipper would take one of the JD 350 dozers and head around one flank, and GT would take the other dozer and head around the other flank. Dynamite and I would each take a side and scout for the best path for the dozers. The fire was moving slowly and only about 18-20 acres by now, but due to the terrain and amount of cedar, you really could not see much more than about the next 10 yards.

I started out and was flagging the route for the dozer to follow. It was slow going, and I kept in constant contact with Dynamite, doing our best to keep track of each other and where the fire was progressing. There was a light wind, and smoke dispersion was extremely poor, topped with the thick, stinging smoke from the greening fescue grass. The closer we got to the head of the fire, the thicker the smoke got. Chipper and GT were making slow progress with the dozers but good progress nonetheless. The flames were less than 2 feet tall, and they were able to plow their line really close to the active fire. Occasionally, they would jump off the dozers and walk back and check their lines to see if the fire had jumped, and call us on the radio and give progress updates. Once we had finished the scouting task, we could then follow up the dozers and burn out and monitor the line, and things would get moving quicker.

By my best guess, I had to be no more than about 100 yards from Dynamite as we were heading toward each other in front of the fire. I called Dynamite on the radio, and while he was talking with me, I heard something different on the radio transmission, then the radio cut out. I called back but got no response. I called again, and after a long pause, I got a response. "I'm OK," but I could tell by his voice that all was not ok. I asked what had happened and if he was truly ok but got no response. The smoke was extremely thick by now, but I started running in his direction, yelling his name out loud. I finally thought I heard something, so I stopped to listen. "Up Here," I heard from slightly up the hill to my left. I started that way and immediately saw a yellow hard hat on the ground. I was wondering what the heck had happened, and by the time I picked up the hard hat, I heard Dynamite say again, "Up Here." I could barely see through the smoke, but I saw him sitting on the ground, holding his head. I rushed up to him and could see blood and bruises all over.

Dynamite had just finished tying a piece of flagging to a cedar branch to mark the proposed dozer line when I called him on the radio. While he was talking to me, he heard something over his right shoulder. He turned to peer through the smoke and saw a dark form brush past him. A white-tailed deer brushed his left side, and he jumped back in reaction. This move put him on a direct path with a deer following up the first deer. Dynamite took the full brunt of the deer square in his chest, and both went sprawling down the slight hill. Between the hit and subsequent fall and the deer pawing around trying to get up, Dynamite received all manner of bumps, bruises, and small cuts. His hard hat flew another 20 yards down the hill, and as quickly as it had happened, the deer disappeared into the thick smoke. Dynamite sat up to collect himself and try to figure out what just happened. He finally heard me shouting for him and answered.

I did a quick assessment of my patient and determined that none of the injuries were very serious. I asked if he could finish, and he said he could finish the fire. I walked back with him along his flag line to meet up with GT and the dozer. Once he was re-established with GT, I made my way back to the scene of the incident. I finished the flag line from where he left off and connected it with mine. I then made my way back to Chipper and the other dozer and began firing out the plow line behind him.

We ended up with no other problems and wrapped the fire up soon thereafter. After we got back to our trucks, we broke open a first aid kit and took care of Dynamite's cuts and scrapes. He was a good sport about the whole ordeal, having to retell the story multiple times. We all had a good, hearty laugh, and while you won't see that incident report on the Wildfire Lessons Learned Web Page, we all remember that fire as the one where "Dynamite got run over by a White Tail!" (We all know you just sang that!)

Sometimes the smoke can be so thick, you never know
what may be running away.

Dynamite creating his own thick smoke on a different fire.

Chapter 5

"Hay Bale" of Fire

Nature is Awesome

I was still fairly new to the area, and the guys were still showing me the ropes in my new district. All I really knew was that the seasoned guys I worked with were saying this fire season was going to be one for the record books. It was late winter of the year, and I had already been able to collect a number of slides of cool and awesome fire behavior I had never seen before. This night was going to be another of those nights.

I was fighting a fire in Hickory County with my crew, Dynamite, GT, and Flash. Like many other fires I had seen the previous fall and now into late winter in West Central Missouri, we would go right on fighting fire into the wee hours of the morning. Well, before we get to those wee hours, I need to back up a bit. The fire we were fighting was in overgrown Eastern Redcedar with blackberries and Serecia lespedeza.

For those who know how Eastern Redcedar, or juniper, burns, you can also make a correlation to how blackberries and serecia burn. There is some resin, or oil in them that makes them almost explosive when a fire runs through them. Anyway, we did not get to this particular fire until very late in the day due to fighting other small fires around the area.

We were unable to even walk through the thick mess of fuel about 3 feet tall and so thick I think even the rabbits had abandoned it for better ground. This got me thinking back to the classic country song, "The Battle of New Orleans," where the lyrics go something like this, "Yeah, they ran through the briars, and they ran through the brambles, and they ran through the bushes where a rabbit couldn't go…" So, since we weren't being chased by Andrew Jackson, there was no point in even trying to walk through to cut a line through it.

We had our trusty dozer on this fire, and this was the only way we could even begin to get a fire line established. Of course, a mere 5-foot dozer line in this fuel and in these burning conditions was not really going to do much with the way the fire was burning, and the wind was blowing.

We were not having much luck with even slowing down this fire, and it was getting along about midnight. The combination of wind and very thick explosive fuels was creating some rather extreme fire behavior. We got a call from dispatch that the winds were about to pick up. Pick Up? "How much faster can they blow?" I was asking myself since I think they were already howling about 40 miles per hour. So, with that, Dynamite gave a call on the radio for everyone to pull back, and we would regroup at the county road to the west.

We got to the road about the time the predicted wind picked up. As I was on a little rise, I had a good view of most of the fire. Dynamite and I stood there discussing our options and talking about the firefight so far when we witnessed the fire make the most impressive run of the day, err, I mean night.

The cedar trees were only about 24-30 feet tall, but with everything in the fuel bed so volatile, the flames were shooting up about 50-60 feet in the air. Every tree was torching and crowning out as the firefront hit it. What we were seeing was a great battle in the laws of nature. The fire was burning so hot and intense that it wanted to shoot flames up over 100 feet if it could, but the wind was blowing so hard, say around 55 mph at the time, that once the flames got so high, the wind took the tips of the flames and bent them over and curled them down. What resulted was the only thing we could use to describe it at the time. The fire was rolling on itself and wrapping up tight in some sort of horizontal vortices, and it really did look like a big round bale of hay, only instead of hay and grass, the bale was made of flames fueled by the highly volatile oils and resins of the fuel.

I asked my trusted tech, Dynamite, if he had ever seen anything like that in his 25+ years of fighting fires. He said no—not even "out West."

We sat watching the awesome show that Mother Nature was putting on for us, knowing there wasn't a single thing we could do to stop it.

Later in my career, I would learn about horizontal roll vortices, personally witness more examples, and see the aftermath of others. But this—this was definitely the first.

As we talked that night, we decided that this was just a random combination of perfect conditions that came together just for us that night on that little rise in West Central Missouri. It was truly a wondrous sight to behold and one I will never forget, especially when I think back to the company I kept that night. Nature is awesome!

Pictures just can't grab the true feeling or emotion of the moment.
But I'll still take the photo anyway and try.

Although not cedar, sometimes the fires can burn with such intensity, they
are just awe-inspiring. What is hard to tell by this photo is that the grass is
thick and about 7-8 foot tall and those flames are reaching 40-50 feet in the
air. I was standing on the seat of an ATV to get this photo.

Chapter 6

I Can Sleep Anywhere

Zzzzzzzzzzzz

Sleep. It can be hard to get sometimes when you are working long and irregular hours. Whether it is running an initial attack in your local district or out on a detail in some other time zone, firefighters are known for working odd hours. For those who know, please bear with me. For those who don't, here is what I am talking about. The call for an initial attack can happen at any hour of the day. In fact, I am pretty sure I have been called out at every hour of the 24-hour day. A call at 4 am is tough in and of itself. You are probably jolted out of your wonderful REM sleep. It can be even harder if you just got home from the last call at 2 am and only had an hour or so of sleep. There are the initial attack fires that roll into extended attacks. Some of these can run 18 to 24 hours, or even up to 40 hours or more before you get a handle on the fire or relief finally gets organized and shows up to take over.

Then, during the details on larger fires, even though there is a bit more stable structure, the hours can still be hard to control. Maybe you are working the night shift. As you try to get some sleep in a hot tent, in a field with no shade, and of course, the wind decided to not blow that day, you suffer in a sweaty realm between dreamland and the reality of the generators blaring. Or maybe you are working a swing shift to get a critical burnout done, and you end your shift after midnight, only to get called out to move to another division to assist with another critical operation. Even working a "normal" day shift does not mean you get 8 hours of restful sleep. The more realistic schedule means you are getting 6 hours at best of decent sleep a night, usually less. Finally, the effects of a long season can have cumulative effects on lack of sleep.

All of this brings me to the topic of this story. Yes, I have learned to sleep anywhere, but more importantly, I have also learned how to grab a few minutes of sleep whenever the opportunity presents itself. Take, for example, a fire in Montana one year. We were there as a crew and getting transported up the mountain in the back of National Guard Deuces. After a long day, I would settle into the pile of gear bags, get really comfortable, and take a nap on the way down the very bumpy, very dusty road. Of course, no one else could sleep in those conditions, so they gave me a hard time, but at least I was getting some rest in.

I have learned how to sleep in a pickup truck, in every seat, and about every position possible. In a pinch, such as when you have not got your tent set up yet and when you are finally ready to go to sleep at 11:30 pm or so, the sky decides to open up and start pouring and even dropping some hail, the driver's seat looks incredibly dry and comfortable. Other times, when you may have more time to rearrange your vehicle, the passenger front seat is a bit better since you don't have the gas and brake pedals or the steering wheel in your way. Of course, if you can get into the back seat of an extended cab truck, you must be living right. However, the best way to sleep in a vehicle, which, sadly, I have not been fortunate enough to experience, is in the back of a minivan with an actual bed mattress in it. I have my wife to thank for telling me how well this works. During our minivan years, we would throw the twin mattress in the back of the van, and she would get to sleep in an actual bed with a roof over her head. It did not matter if it was very dusty, rainy, cold, or hot; she had pretty good sleeping conditions for her Public Information Officer (PIO) duties. She, and a good PIO friend of ours, refer to this as Linear Condos.

Before I learned about the wonders of vehicle sleeping or even sleeping in a tent, I mastered the basics of sleeping out under the stars. Sleeping out under the stars is something I had a leg up on from way back to my years in Boy Scouts. While we would usually set up tents, Boy Scouts did a good job of preparing you for whatever may come along. This meant actual campouts where we purposely left the tents behind. We would need to make our own improvised shelters or just learn to use our sleeping bag and an old surplus wool army blanket to survive the night. However, my most fond memories were not of actual Scout-sponsored outings. See, we had a couple of years where some of the scout parents missed the part of preparing their young boys for the harsh realities of life. If it looked like it might rain, they made a fuss, and the campout got canceled. Or, maybe it was going to be too cold for their fragile little boy to handle, again, a canceled campout. This, of course, did not sit well with some of us slightly older scouts.

One of my best friends growing up, Craig, would offer up his dad's farm for our "unofficial" campout, and along with another of my best friends, Jeff, we went and spent the night or the weekend anyway, regardless of the rain, or cold, or whatever other excuse was offered for the canceled campout. It was actually on these night outs that I learned so many of the tricks for sleeping under the stars that I used later in the deserts of Arizona, the mountains of Montana and Oregon, or on the sage steppe of

Wyoming. One key is to find the right height for your head. Not always having a pillow, you learn what size rock or log works. Ok, ok, just a rock leaves me with an intense headache in the morning, so on one of those early campouts, I learned that a properly folded t-shirt makes just enough padding to prevent said headache. Later, on one of many fires, I figured out how to stuff a pair of leather work gloves to provide just the right amount of padding for my pillow.

While I may have upgraded to a low-profile, lightweight cot as my bones don't like the hard ground as much anymore, I still grab a chance to sleep under the stars on occasion. On one particular fire, a group of us Division and Ops folks would leave camp and drive about 5 minutes out into the middle of some BLM ground and just sort of scatter about. I would throw my cot either in the bed of the pickup or on the ground and fall asleep to the stars. Only the threat of rain would make me pop the tent.

Like many folks have come to realize, we should have enjoyed those naps in kindergarten a little more because we don't seem to get enough naps as adults. However, I have learned that even a 3-minute nap has an amazing power to re-energize you on a long fire or long assignment. There have been times when the only place to sit and rest was ashes about 6 inches deep, but I could still get that 3-minute nap.

Finally, I wanted to relay a couple of the better sleeping arrangements I have had dealing with fires. Coming in at second place, there was a crew assignment for initial attack in Minnesota, where we were in a hotel room every night, right on the shore of Lake Superior. A shower, a hot meal at the neighboring restaurant, and a hotel bed with a view of the lake every night can be pretty hard to beat for a fire assignment. However, I think this next one takes first place for me. While working as the Night

Operations Chief on a Type 3 fire, I was offered a bedroom in a local house. Now, I don't know the details of how or why. Frankly, I don't care. All I know is that working the night shift and trying to sleep during the day is next to impossible. With this setup, I had a private farmhouse bedroom with my own bathroom for a shower. The windows had really dark shades on them, so I could get the room pretty much black even during the middle of the day, and it was air-conditioned.

The owners were wonderful people and just so thankful that we were there. They even had a fresh batch of warm cookies on a plate for me each afternoon when I woke before I left the house to go on shift. I think every future night shift will forever be ruined because of those sleeping arrangements.

Now, we put night shift firefighters in hotels, bring in specially designed "sleep trailers," or designate some air-conditioned dark room at a local school so that they can get better quality sleep. But the older firefighters will definitely remember the challenges of sleeping.

Alas, as I get older, I am still perfecting the art of being able to sleep anywhere. I think my favorite is now on my reclining couch, sitting next to my wife, in the middle of a weekend afternoon, a movie on.......zzzzzzzzzz.

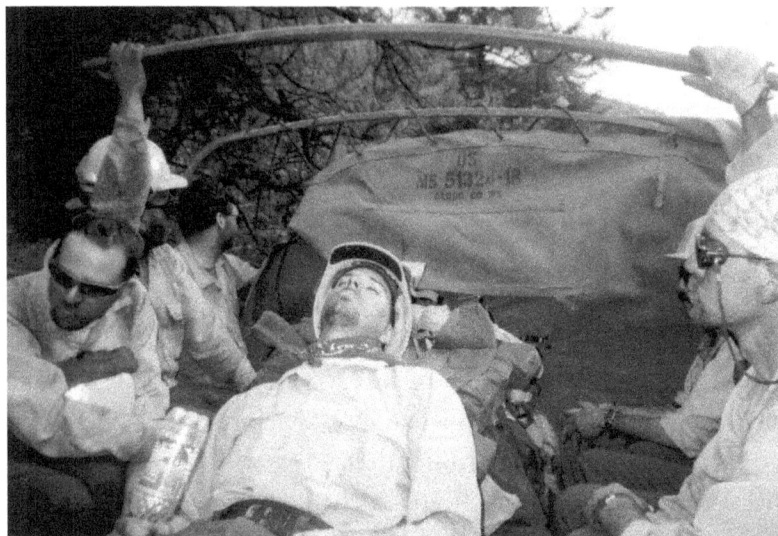

Photo of me sleeping in the back of the Deuce and a Half after a long day on the mountain. I don't know who stole my camera and took the photo, as I didn't know this photo existed until I got home and had my film rolls developed.

In the middle of nowhere, under the stars, at last light, yeah, good sleeping.

Chapter 7

Cat Tracks

Feeling a Little Exposed?

I was on a fire in central Washington as a Task Force Leader. This was a fairly small fire by large fire standards that year in the state, only about 3,000 acres or so, and I have to say, I was pretty surprised that there was even a Type 2 Team on it, given the dozens of other larger fires and complexes all throughout the state. There were also not a whole lot of resources assigned to the fire, maybe a couple hundred or so. This allowed for some pretty quiet operational periods and a feeling of being somewhat isolated in some sections of the fire.

I had a pretty evenly spread mix of resources assigned to my task force. There were 2 T2IA hand crews, 2 T6 Engines, 2 fallers with a Felling Boss, and 2 Dozers with a Dozer Boss. Anyway, the fire wasn't moving much, and the area of our responsibility was pretty spread out. I had the engines patrolling about a mile and a half of the road while the hand crews were mopping up a section of line through some rocks. The fallers were snagging out behind the dozers who were cutting some contingency line. Overall, I had a lot of ground to cover, and to walk in along the actual fire line took quite a while.

After a few days, I thought I would change up my routine and cut through a burned area and cut my walk time in half to get to where the crews were working. This route took an old trail up and over a fairly steep ridge and then through some timber that had not completely burned. I don't know what was different about this particular day, but something was a little twisted. Maybe it was the powdered eggs from breakfast or the extra chocolate milk I grabbed on my way out of the mess tent. Either way, I knew the trail through the middle of the burn would be secluded, and I could stop along the way to take care of business.

As I was about a third of the way down the trail, I really had to go. The twisted feeling had turned to all manner of gurgling and other obnoxious noises. I started looking for a good rock to go behind or at least a decent tree stump that hadn't burned completely. About this time, I looked down and noticed a nice, fresh, large mountain lion track in the ashes! Oh, this created a dilemma! See, I really had to "drop a load," but I also now knew a large cat was somewhere in the area as well. Now, normally, this knowledge wouldn't bother me, as I am a tough firefighter, right? I have my Pulaski for backup as well. But just the thought of having my pants down made me feel a bit "vulnerable." I kept heading down the trail. The problem was the cat tracks kept going that way as well.

A few hundred yards further, and I noticed tracks head off the trail just to come back to the trail later. And I REALLY needed to go. I felt like I was about to mess my pants. So, with that, I did find a smallish boulder to lean up against while I did my thing. I looked around, took off my pack, looked around, positioned my Pulaski, looked around, got my toilet paper out of my pack, looked around, and kicked some excess ash out of my way. Oh, did I mention I looked around? The moment of truth was upon me. With my head on a swivel, I unbuttoned my pants. Slowly, I pulled them down and started getting into my squat. The whole time, my head was going from one side to the other, just waiting for the cat to take advantage of my moment of complete helplessness.

I have to admit, I have never felt more "exposed" than I did right then. We read about the mountain men fighting off bears and other heroic feats, but I don't recall reading about them doing this while their pants were down. My head never stopped moving as I worked it out and finished up, and I think I even gained some air when I straightened up so fast while pulling up my pants. I quickly got my pack back on and my hands back on my Pulaski. Whew! Now I feel a lot better. I am back to being a man, a formidable foe if this cat comes calling, not some piece of prey with his lily-white backside fully exposed.

With that done, I hurried down the trail and finally got to where I needed to be. I never did see the cat, but a crew in a neighboring Division did report a mountain lion the next day. The whole rest of the fire, I decided to keep this little bit of information about my hike to myself. Only when I got back home did the story come out. A good laugh, even at my own expense, is always a good thing.

Yep, direct evidence of an unwanted visitor to the trail.

Of course, you never know what else may be watching you,
ready to pounce in a moment of weakness.

Chapter 8

Mending Fence

The Best Fence on the Farm

We run fire dozers a lot in Missouri. Early in my career, it was the John Deere 350 fire dozers that had cages welded to the cab, and in addition to the small blade up front, we had fire plows on the rear. These were small and nimble and could navigate the woods of the Ozarks pretty well. The fastest way to use them was to drop the plow and go, weaving around the larger trees but trying to keep as straight a line as possible. I will admit these plows could make a pretty deep line in the right soil, so we started modifying them into low-impact plows. These would not cut as deep but would actually make a wider line by moving the resulting dirt farther away. Wider lines are better in our line of work, and we still have the nimbleness of the small dozers.

Of course, any good thing can come to an end, and John Deere decided that they were no longer going to make this small model. We started getting into the 400 series and then the 450 series. Each time we got a new series, the machine got bigger. That required a bigger transport, and that required a different CDL licensing. It was so nice to have a single rear axle 2-ton truck with a roll-back bed to haul the 350s on. The guys could get closer to the fires as they could navigate the small roads better and

41

turn around better. As for the transports for the larger machines, we had a Ford F-550 hauling a large gooseneck trailer.

Heavier machines and larger transports also meant we were now over the limit on many bridges around the district. This just added a layer to the complexity, as we had to know which side of the creek a fire was on before the dozer guys could roll because they could not cross the bridge in some of our high-fire areas.

Also, with the larger machines, the front blades got wider as well. It was getting harder and harder to navigate through the woods. Yes, you could push over larger trees, but you still have limits, and you really didn't want to be causing that much damage to the resource anyway.

No matter the time period, using dozers on fires meant we had to cut fences when we encountered them. We would always look for a gate or gap in the fence where possible. The guys would cut line right up to the fence, pick up the blade or plow, go down through the gate, come back, and start again. We would construct the short section of hand line where the fence was. Unfortunately, this was not always the case. Some places seemed to have a mile of fence with no gaps or gates, and we would have to cut it to keep doing what we were doing. We always came back when we were done and fixed the fence. We carried wire pullers, extra wire, staples, and any other tools we needed for the job of fixing the fence.

Most landowners or farmers were very understanding; some even told us not to worry about it. They would fix it themselves and were happy to have the fire out. Sometimes, I think they just didn't trust us to do it right. I mean, what can a firefighter know about fences, right? On the other hand, there were some who would complain no matter what when we cut a fence. What were we thinking? Why did we cut it there? We didn't fix it right. You know the drill.

Well, I can tell you. My guys knew how to fix a fence. They all had a farming and cattle background and had fixed miles of fences not only on fires but also on their own places and neighbors. These guys knew what to look for and when it was absolutely necessary to cut a fence.

One example, the fence was fairly loose and a bit saggy when we cut it. When the fire was over, and they came back to fix it, the wires were tight, if not tighter than when it was first installed. Kind of going back to the saying, "Leave it better than you found it."

Another time, on a day in late July when the temperature was about 112 degrees, we were on our second fire of the day. Being short-staffed and with the heat, we relied on the dozers to cut the lines. If we didn't have the dozer, it would have taken three times as many people as I had about 3 hours longer to get the fire worked on. I got a call from one of my dozer operators about an irate landowner, and could I come over to talk with him? I drove around and finally find the landowner. Before I could even say a word, the barrage of insults and cussing started. I won't get into exactly what was said, but it was not nice. This went on for what seemed like five minutes.

He finally took a breath and was about to start again when I cut him off with a "Are you done yet?" This seems to derail him, and he fumbles for a response. This was the opening I needed. Now, realize that at this point in my life, I had gotten better about my foul mouth and didn't cuss that much anymore. However, and this is not a proud moment, I feel I used the appropriate cuss words to punctuate my statements pretty well. See, I just had to "speak his language" and explain the situation to him. This was the hottest day of the year. This was not the first fire of the day. I had already sent one firefighter to the hospital for heat exhaustion. We were indeed going to use this dozer to fight this fire. I would be happy to call the sheriff myself, as he said he was going to do. Since I had a suspicion that he caused the fire, but I didn't want to come out and accuse him, maybe he needed to tone it down a bit. Maybe, just maybe, he should rethink his whole stance and work with us. Like, maybe tell us if there was a gap in the fence or a gate that we could go through.

On the one hand, I kind of wish someone had a video of that speech I gave, as I feel I was firing on all cylinders and using his language so he could understand. But, on the other hand, I'm glad there is no proof, as I would probably be pretty embarrassed by the language I used. In the end, with his train of thought adjusted, he was actually a pretty helpful guy. He showed us the gaps and gates and the best places to tie into other trials. He led our dozer over miles of line and did a rather good job. When we did have to cut the fence in one particular spot, he cut the fence himself and helped us when it was time to fix it. He even called me the next day to discuss how to mop up some hot spots and to apologize for his behavior the previous day.

My final example was on a fire in a high fire area. It seemed as though the place burned about every other year, and the property we stopped it on, the old farmer, was just grateful to have us there. Over the years and number of fires, many of the wooden posts had burned, and most of the fence was down and in bad shape. On this particular fire, the line was right through the only part of the fence that was still standing. We looked at going up or down the fence, but the terrain and steep slopes prevented that from happening. So, we did what needed to be done. After the fire was contained and we are tracking the dozer back out, we stop and fix the fence. Again, better than we found it.

Jump to the next day, and I got a call at the office. Mr. Land-owner's son was back in the area and livid about what had happened. I'm not usually one to take much, especially over the phone, where anonymity allows a bolder approach. I offered to come back out and meet him on-site to discuss his concerns. When I arrive, his temper was, well, tempered a bit. Face-to-face either calms folks down or emboldens them. I was fortunate to have the calmer version of the son. We discussed the ins and outs of why here, what we did to improve the spot, and everything else. He was not really happy, no matter what I said. With that, I tell him to walk with me. We go 200 yards in one direction, where the fence was mostly down and in poor repair. We go the other direction about 200 yards to where it was also in disrepair, as it went through the holler. He started to get a bit quieter as I point all this out.

As we got back to the fire line and where we had fixed the fence, the older landowner was there. This was just what the son needed to get a bit fired back up, and he started cussing me again about the poor job we did. It was at this time that the "dad" told his son to shut the heck up! This was the best fence on the entire farm! Maybe he could take a lesson from us and get to work on the rest of the fences. The son didn't say another word, and the landowner smiled at me, said thanks again, and said sorry for the inconvenience of dealing with his "know nothing" son.

One of the later dozers we had, but still early enough to have
a fire plow on the rear.

One of the little 350 fire dozers with a plow. Chipper is pushing
some drift buildup in the Truman Lake bottoms.

46

Chapter 9

Bearings and Chains

Understanding our Terminology

We use a lot of specific jargon in the firefighting world and in the forestry world, for that matter. Add to that the fact that jargon can differ greatly across the country, and sometimes, even firefighters can have a hard time understanding each other. Growing up, one of my favorite writers, Patrick McManus, had the Hunters Dictionary, where he offered further explanations of common hunting terms and phrases for the reader. So, with that, I offer my version of the firefighter's dictionary. Like any good deck of cards, enjoy these 52 terms and phrases, Bearings and Chains.

BURN OUT - see also Back Fire, the art of igniting the fuels right next to a fire break or fire line so as to burn out the remaining fuels between that fire line and the main fire. This makes the fire line wider, and the fire intensity is generally lower and easier to handle than the main fire.

BACKFIRE - see also Burn Out; both of these terms are used interchangeably in many areas, but alas, leave it to lawyers and politicians to complicate things. Without a full, boring, and sometimes confusing back history, just know that at some point along the line, we were to only use burnout as the correct term unless a very specific set of criteria were met, and then we could use the term backfire or backfiring.

BEARINGS - Refers to getting a bearing in regard to your location and terrain. More specifically, a reading on a compass as you navigate the wilds of remote fires or a visual grasp of the general terrain and direction you may be heading.

CHAINS - A unit of measurement from the old days when the country was first settled and surveyed for the first time. 1 chain equals 66 feet and is made up of 100 links. There are 80 chains in a mile. Mop-up standards were usually talked about in chains, such as "mop-up all heat out to 2 chains." If a crew was digging a line to keep the crew motivated, it was often shouted out that there were "only 2 more chains!" That sounds so much better than 132 feet or the half-mile that it actually was.

MOP-UP - Once the fire is contained within the fire breaks, firefighters work to extinguish all the heat and hot spots to extinguish the flames and smoldering. When used with water, this is wet mop-up, and without water is dry mop-up. Mop-up can also be referred to as clean or dirty mop-up and has to do with how completely the fire burned in that area. As firefighters like to get dirty, they always prefer to get the dirty mop-up assignments.

DOZER - Any of a range of tracked machines that are used to clear fuels to create a fire break. Today, all makes and models are used, but the most beloved was the small JD350 with an open-air cab and steel rods welded on to create a safety cage for the operator.

PLOW - An attachment that is pulled behind the dozer that digs into the ground and not only removes all fuels but also slings dirt to each side, therefore creating a wider fire break. There have been hundreds of designs over the years that included deep furrows, lower impact furrows, some with wheels, and some without.

BLADE - The big, mostly flat, steel part of the front of a dozer that is used to push trees, brush, and other fuels away to create a fire break. These come in various sizes, usually dictated by the size of the dozer it is attached to.

LEAF RAKE - A regular-looking rake, but made with tempered round spring steel tines that are used to clean up your yard and be the envy of your neighbors, as their cheap plastic rakes are always breaking. A secondary use is by firefighters to move leaves and small branches off the ground to create a fire line through the forest. It can also be used to "drag fire" by stabbing a lot of leaves onto the tines and, as those leaves burn, dragging them along the fire line to ignite your burnout, although without as much "coolness factor" as the person with the drip torch.

LEAF BLOWER - A large, extremely noisy engine and tube you usually wear on your back to blow leaves and debris off your sidewalk or driveway and annoy your neighbors as you get an early start to your weekend by starting your yard clean-up at 5 a.m. to beat the heat. A secondary use is to blow leaves and small branches down to bare soil to create a fire break in the forest of oaks and hickories. One leaf blower can take the place of at least 3 well-trained firefighters using only leaf rakes, who usually look at the guy with the leaf blower with disdain, and jealousy as he or she is taking their job away from them.

DRIP TORCH - An aluminum fuel can with a cloth wick on the end that you intentionally light on fire, with the express intent of allowing that burning wick to ignite the fuel in the can as you pour it out on the ground. Not to be confused with a Molotov cocktail. As for the fuel inside, it depends on who you work for as to what "mix" it should be (required), but as most firefighters are a bit crazy anyway, everyone has their own special mix that they swear only they can use and no one else as it is too "hot" for anyone to use. Drip torches are highly effective at putting the right amount of fire on the ground to ignite a burnout, a backfire, or any part of an ignition sequence for a prescribed fire.

YELLOWS – Generally referring to the Nomex shirts that most firefighters would wear. Nomex is actually a trade name for a fire-resistant material. While there are now all sorts of colors of fire-resistant materials that are worn, such as red, blue, and tan, the vast majority are still yellow.

HOLLER - n. Also, ravine, as in a steep drainage in the terrain that may or may not be crossable with equipment such as dozers.

HOLLER - v. as in yelling. If the radios were not working correctly, one crew member may holler to the next to relay messages.

JUST A SHORT HIKE - Not a short hike. Be sure you pack a double lunch and extra snacks to get you through.

BIRD – aircraft, usually a helicopter, but can also include a number of different planes or jets. Also, ship.

BIG ERNIE - Mostly of western lore, but has crept into all regions where wildfires happen. A fire god of sorts that would control the overall destiny of a wildfire and the firefighters fight them.

FIRE DEMON – As in the Truman Lake Fire Demon. It could also be akin to karma, dragons, or Big Ernie. An unknown, unseen entity that seemed to control the amount of fortune, good or bad that a firefighter would experience.

KARKHAGNE - as described by the Missouri Chapter of the Society of American Foresters, is a mythical beast that was reported to roam the forests of Missouri in the past century. It is covered by fur, feathers, scales, and armor plate, has a diet of limestone section corners, and can quickly escape humans or other carnivorous pursuers by completely engulfing itself within the recesses of its own hip pocket. It is the subject of considerable folklore and legends about forestry in Missouri in the early twentieth century. The Karkhagne not only symbolizes the importance of Missouri's forests to all creatures, but it also represents the unique and sometimes harsh nature of forestry at the turn of the last century. Read the following article from the University of Missouri Log in 1964 for more lore. Woods, Ed. 1964. **The Karkhagne** Missouri Log 17:34-36.

I'LL MEET YOU AT THE DROP POINT IN 5 MINUTES - There is no intention of being there in five minutes, and you will probably not see them for the next 3 hours.

DROP POINT - A point on a map designated by a number, for instance, DP51, not to be confused with Area 51. However, on the ground, at the actual drop point, there can be all manner of weird and unexplainable activities, like "We delivered all your lunches to the drop point 2 hours ago; we don't know why they are missing now."

ROLLING – This could be a fire really running hard, or wheels turning on a truck or engine, or the almost uncontrollable laughter from fellow crew members when an individual did something stupid like they can't find the inversion lifter.

SLIDES – generally a term used to imply gained experience. Long ago, early photos were taken on slide film and made into small, paper-bound holders that were then put into a slide carousel and then in a projector. When a light was shown through the slide, it was projected in a wall or screen. When an individual had a lot of experience, they had a lot of slides to show at training. Therefore, if you gained some valuable lesson or experience, you added that slide to the carousel.

SEAT – Single Engine Air Tanker, think crop duster or Dusty Crop Hopper. These are piloted by the most daring of pilots. I wonder if "crazy" is a requirement on the job sheet.

SHIP – aircraft, also bird, as in "get the ship up for some bucket work."

FENCE – wires of any age and any condition, usually used to either keep something in, like livestock, or something out, like you. Regardless of the condition or appearance, if a fire runs through it, the owner of such a fence will declare it was the best fence in the county.

FIRE PATROL - general term used to define riding in a small bird, think Cessna 182, looking for smoke on the horizon and then performing all manner of acrobatics and tight circles to see how fast the pilot could make the spotter regret eating lunch, breakfast, and possibly even that gas station sushi from 3 days ago.

THE BOTTOMS - The collective area of the lower elevation and mostly flat parts of the Truman Lake flood plain that is now covered in dead trees and annual weeds. In wet years, the bottoms would be flooded and covered in water or mud, while in drought years, they were covered in annual weeds and grasses and the remaining dead trees or snags. A local hot spot for firebugs and arsonists.

PULASKI - A combination tool named for Forester Edwin Pulaski that was the best of both the axe and hoe, all in one tool. While not invented by Ed Pulaski, he did tinker with the design and is ultimately the one whose name was applied to the tool. Pulaski was one of the heroes of the Big Blowup Fires of 1910. The Pulaski tool is still used by firefighters today.

A-10 - An absolutely awesome beast of a close-support military attack fighter jet. All soldiers cheer when it shows up at a battle. Firefighters doing a prescribed fire operation, not so much.

WOODS - Any area that has trees. This could be the vast pine, spruce, and fir forests that cover the mountainsides of the West, the oak-hickory forests of the East and Midwest, or the cypress swamps of the South. Also, a forester and firefighters' normal stomping grounds. Sometimes also referred to as the backwoods.

THE AGENCY - Generally referred to as the employing agency of the firefighter at the time of the story.

MDC - Missouri Department of Conservation. The employing agency for many of the stories listed here.

FED - Also Federal Agency, Fed is shorthand for any federal firefighter, no matter who they work for. Common federal agencies include the US Forest Service (USFS), Bureau of Land Management (BLM), National Park Service (NPS), Fish and Wildlife Service (FWS), Bureau of Indian Affairs (BIA), and potentially others.

TYPE 6 ENGINE - Engines are typed based on things like how many people staff the engine, water capacity, pump capacity, and other such metrics. Type 6 engines are the smallest officially recognized and standardized of the engines. These can be on a ton-and-a-half chassis like the Ford F-550 or a similar-sized truck.

TYPE 7 ENGINE - Generally considered anything smaller than a Type 6. In the case of most of Missouri, they use half-ton and ¾ ton pickup trucks with a small water tank, usually 100 gallons, along with a 5 hp, high-pressure/low-volume pump.

TENDER - A truck that carries water to help resupply engines, drop tanks, or any other needs for the firefighting efforts. Sometimes also referred to as Tankers.

TANKER - In some parts of the country, this refers to a truck that helps resupply water to engines. While this can and does create confusion, depending on where a firefighter is from and where they may be. It should be noted that the more official definition of tanker is for a bird or ship as an aerial vehicle that drops water or retardant. Also, air tankers (as in Single Engine Air Tankers or Heli-tanker)

IC - Incident Commander, the person who has the overall responsibility for a particular wildfire. This could be an Initial Attack IC on a very small fire, an Extended Attack IC on a longer duration fire, or a Type 2 or Type 1 IC on the largest and most complex fires. Currently, the Type 1 and 2 ICs are rolled into Complex Incident Commander.

TOWERMAN - a person who staffs the fire tower and can be either male or female. While not required, the following traits are helpful to fulfill the job duties of a Towerman: rough, gruff, dry humor and a pretty refined run of sarcasm, long scraggly beards are encouraged, and that goes for the guys, too. Appearing too out of shape to climb the steps to the cabin but then being able to outclimb anyone who shows up, all the while unleashing a barrage of well-timed insults and wisecracks to the newcomer who dared think differently.

CABIN (Tower) - the small building on top of the tower and steps that is nothing but a roof with windows, a small table, a stool, and a fire finder, all cramped into a spot barely large enough for 1 person. Some cabins in the west or more mountainous areas, especially those owned by federal agencies, could be considered luxurious as they not only served as the lookout but also home to the towerman or lookout. These could be up to 14 or more feet squared and have a bed or 2, couches, chairs, and a small kitchen as well.

CABIN (structure) - The building that serves the owner as either a primary residence in the back woods of the forests, a second home to the more well-to-do, or a hunting cabin for hunters. Some cabins can be historic and worth millions of dollars. Some are worth mere pennies, that is, until they burn up, then they are worth millions.

HUNKER - Also, hunkering, the art of being gainfully employed but not being found. There are times when you have mopped up the same section of the fire line so many times, and it has been so long since the last hot spot was found that new trees and grass are starting to grow again. But you are told to "do it again," so you go back and do your job so well that any overhead that comes by not only can't find any heat but also can't find you.

LCES - official, Lookouts, Communication, Escape Route, Safety Zone, the 4 main things each firefighter should be sure are in place and know before engaging in a firefight. Unofficial, Locate Cooler Establish Shade, the critical elements of a crew when hunkering is the task for the day

HOT SPOT - also heat; this could be creeping or smoldering fire in duff or stump holes, hot rocks, or just about anything that potentially could start a new fire or allow an escape of the existing fire. Hot spots are generally small spots of heat, like the aforementioned examples.

HEAT - also hot spot. Sometimes differentiated from hot spots due to specific circumstances. Heat may refer to a generalized area that could be a few square feet.

OVER YONDER - Any distance measured from feet to miles to indicate where some overhead is headed or coming from. This could be just across the holler or on the other side of a mountain range, two states away.

COLD TRAILING - a method of mop-up that requires you to use your bare, un-gloved hand to feel that everything is cold to the touch and that you find no heat or hot spots. It is also the preferred method to ensure you get the dirtiest hands possible. This is to build a layer of protective dirt and ash so that you can eat your cold burrito or ham sandwich without washing your hands.

OVERHEAD - Can refer to any next-level supervisor. For a crew or engine, it may be the crew boss or engine boss. This will also include task force leaders, division supervisors, safety officers, ops chiefs, or really anyone up the chain of command.

CAMP RAT - Reserved for some select overhead positions that seem to never leave camp, can shower in the middle of the day, and have both heated and air-conditioned tents to work in while the actual firefighters go do all the dirty work.

INVERSION LIFTER - A critically important tool used by experienced engine crews to lift the weather inversion that has settled in over the fire for the past 3 days. It is only a pure coincidence that the engine captain and senior firefighters are too busy to grab it themselves and ask the rookie to hurry and bring it up.

HOSE JOCKEY - A voluntold beginning firefighter, often in their first year, told to carry large quantities of hose and other similar equipment to a drop point several hundred feet up the mountain. Only to find a road at the top.

IMPASSABLE ROAD - Any road that gives the slightest indication that it may mar the paint on the vehicle being driven by any overhead.

PRACTICALLY A 4-LANE HIGHWAY - A road of questionable existence or substance that may have most recently been used by a small herd of deer and is now only passable by a type 6 and a terrified engine crew. Often said to be 'only rough in a spot or two,' but proceeds to shake all manner of bolts loose. Speeds upwards of 55mph can be achieved only when the boss isn't looking. Hey! Where did the pump go?

One of the many fires we had in "the bottoms" of the
Truman Lake zone.

Chapter 10

The 40 Hour Run

Can you say Delirium?

The dreaded 40-hour run. Yes, I am talking about fighting fires for 40 hours or more straight. Do we like to do it? No. Is it supposed to happen? No. Is it fun? No. Does it happen anyway? Yes. Actually, I have had a small handful of these 40-hour runs in my career. Three, to be exact, with a number of others between the 24- and 36-hour mark. Thankfully, I think those days are behind me, and I won't have anymore. We have more safety procedures in place these days, and where I am now, there are lots more firefighters to relieve the initial attack forces.

One particular run was really 42 hours. It started out innocent enough. The first fire was early, about 9 am, and nothing to really speak of. A small fire that was probably lit the night before, but no one noticed, and it was not really moving very well. A couple of hours on this one, and we had it wrapped up. By then, there were others going, and we were sent to the nearest fire to get started fighting that one. A quick dozer line and burnout around that one, and we were done. After we got that one mopped up and were sitting around shooting the bull on the tailgate, I got a call to go to a neighboring district an hour away to help with yet another fire. It was well after dark before I arrived, and we worked the fire all night. Shortly before daybreak, we got it wrapped up enough that I was released to head home.

About 10 minutes from my house, I saw a glow of fire North of the road I was on and in an area that sometimes burns. At the same time, there was a sprinkle of rain, enough that I had to turn on my wipers. Good, I thought. Let the rain have this one. Literally, as I got to my driveway, I was called to another fire 20 minutes South of me. The sun was coming up by now, and I started to get a second wind.

Having the light of day was a boost to help keep me going, although, with the morning light, I saw that the clouds were disappearing. No more rain for us. This fire took until early afternoon. As we were getting this one mostly wrapped up, the call came from the spotter plane that a fire was really rolling and needed attention. Can you guess which one that would be? Yep, the fire about 10 minutes north of my house that I saw earlier. There was not enough rain to help, and now, with the heat of the day and winds picking up, she was off to the races!

Another of the crew was already looking to gain access to this fire but was having trouble finding the right trail or a gate through a fence. We met up and finally figured out the route. As we would need a dozer to do anything with this fire and the closest dozer was still 30 minutes out, I went back and flagged the route and then started scouting one side of the fire to try to get some idea of where would be best to start the dozer, while the other guy scouted the other side.

By this time, I was getting pretty tired and hungry. I had already cleaned out my stash of emergency food consisting of pop-top cans of fruit, tuna, and some packages of jerky. This was also in the days before I drank coffee, not that I had any available anyway. What I wouldn't do for a can of Mountain Dew! Just something with some caffeine!

I will be honest; my recollections have been a bit blurry. I do remember at some point about sundown, someone showed up with a few boxes of pizza for the 5 or 6 of us there. After a quick bite to eat, we were able to finally get a line around the entire fire and start the mop-up process. As there was no relief to come, give us a break; we just kept at it. All of us were a bit punchy come midnight, and we made sure to team up on any snags that needed cutting just to keep an extra set of bloodshot, droopy eyes watching out for each other.

You hear stories of people seeing things or hallucinating when they become so exhausted, and that was happening to us. Again, a bit fuzzy, but I clearly remember an owl laughing and making fun of me and a raccoon waddling by carrying a piece of pizza. When I said, "Hey! That's not for you," he just shrugged and said, "Well, you weren't there to stop me." It was also on this night, one of only 2 times in my life, that I thought I caught a glimpse of the Karkhagne, the legendary beast that roams the forests of Missouri. Actually, come to think of it, the other time was also at the tail end of a 40-hour run. Oh, but that must just be a mere coincidence.

Even now, I don't remember how, but we must have finished up that fire and got everyone loaded up and headed home. I don't actually remember driving home. I do have a recollection of the thought process of not showering when I got home. Usually, no matter what, when I got home, I showered before I crawled into bed. On this particular night, I didn't have the energy and just plopped down in my chair in the front room. My wife heard me come in and figured I would shower and be right to bed. When I didn't come in after a few minutes, she got up to check on me and found me asleep in the front room, boots still on. She told me later it was 3am when I came home. So ended a 42-hour run of fires, and having been awake for 44 hours.

This happened during one of those years when we just ran from fire to fire for days and weeks on end. Every one of us in the district were doing the best we could do to mitigate fatigue. Some fires were fought alone or with one other, while some of the most ferocious ended up taking all of us, plus neighboring districts, plus a large number of volunteers from the local fire departments. Everyone in the community was tired.

I could relate the other 40-hour runs if I could remember the details, of course. I know when and where they happened due to notes at the time of the fire reports and of shared stories with those who shared the experience. However, just recalling the story above has me tired and a bit fuzzy, and a cat also just walked by and said he was out of the mouse-catching business; call someone else. I don't have a cat anymore. Haven't for about 12 years. Can you say Delirium?

Is the cat really tying my boots? Or maybe just being generally unhelpful?
Or am I so delirious that I'm dreaming the whole thing?
Photo by Tammy Shroyer

Chapter 11

Truman Lake Fire Demon

As it was with our tight-knit crew in West Central Missouri, working many long hours together, fighting fires in the same areas year after year, we found ourselves talking of things that seemed "otherworldly." What was really controlling our destiny? Was it God guiding our steps? Was there such a thing as karma? Did Big Ernie really control the lightning bolts that flew from the sky? Our discussion covered the whole range of possibilities, but as with any group that had a ton of camaraderie, we decided that we would create our own legend of the area.

With the uniqueness of the Truman Lake area and all the flood-killed timber that burned so frequently, we discussed the possibilities of naming this legend. And so, it came to pass that in 2006, I wrote down the story that would become the Truman Lake Fire Demon. The precipitating event for all this was the upcoming retirement of my Uncle Rich, or Ranger Rich, as everyone knew him, and I wanted to create something truly unique to give him at his celebration. He had worked on the Truman Project for the past 34 years as a forester and fought hundreds of wildfires in the area. He was my inspiration for becoming a forester and firefighter in the first place.

The leaf rakes we used so much would eventually become bent and twisted, the handles would be scorched and burnt, and sometimes break. An idea came to mind to transform this tool into a representation of a lifetime of work. With the help of one of my trusted technicians, we crafted the first relic of the fire demon. Overall, only a small handful were given out, less than a dozen for sure.

With that, I wanted to share the story, as given to a trusted friend and mentor, when he was presented with his relic of the Truman Lake Fire Demon. Mike was a tough supervisor, and it seemed like we butted heads often. However, I came to understand he was just preparing me for other parts of life still ahead. I would grow frustrated when I kept having to justify something in our budget or give reasons why a project would not be completed in time. I would come to learn that, as painful as that process was, once I "convinced" Mike, he would go to bat for us with the higher-ups. And he usually won. If he didn't, we knew that there was just no way. Anyway, Mike became a very close friend of mine, and I consider him one of my better mentors.

Sadly, Mike is no longer with us, but he helped make me into who I am today, and so I wanted to share the "award" we gave him.

Truman Lake Fire Demon

Lurking throughout West Central Missouri, specifically, the haunts surrounding Truman Lake (I know, it's really a reservoir, but hey, this is my story), is a small yet enduring presence. This may take many forms, from an unnoticed wisp of a summer breeze to a howling ferocious wind of an early March storm. From a dark, moonless winter night as black as death itself to a blazing hot July day with nary a cloud in the sky. What I speak of has never been seen by any living soul, but the reports of its whereabouts could fill volumes. It keeps track of all who try to find it. It takes an individual's blood, sweat, and tears through many years to even learn of its existence. And, when this demon finally decides that a select individual is worthy to know that they were, indeed, a contender in this grand eternal fight, it leaves behind a marker. This marker, a relic really, may take years to be found, and then only by someone who has been given the marker before. This burned, rusted, twisted mass of days past starts out as a treasured piece of our critical equipment. It is taken without our knowledge and transformed on an anvil made up of long hours and late nights, hammered by the blood that was given, twisted by the sweat and tears that were shed, and finally formed into the prize that, amongst a small group, brings utter delight. When this marker, this rare relic, is found and given to the one who earned it, if they listen really close to the trees, the grasses, and the wind, they may hear the demon speak. It will say, "I am the Truman Lake Fire Demon. I was put here by God to test your mettle, and you have proven yourself a valiant protector of this beautiful land. Be ever vigilant as this struggle will continue, but know that you have earned a respected place in this wonderful, natural world."

Presented to Mike Huffman, November 1, 2014,
Josh Shroyer, 2006

This is generally how the Truman Lake Fire Demon is found.

Photo of Mike that I took while he was watching the Lost Valley Hatchery
Prescribed Burn. I think he really liked this photo as
he kept it on the wall in his office.

Truman Lake Fire Demon

Lurking throughout West Central Missouri, specifically the haunts surrounding Truman Lake (I know, it's really a reservoir, but hey, this is my story), is a small, yet enduring presence. This may take many forms; from an un-noticed wisp of a summer breeze, to a howling ferocious wind of an early March storm. From a dark, moonless winter night as black as death itself, to a blazing hot July day with nary a cloud in the sky. What I speak of has never been seen by any living soul, but the reports of its whereabouts could fill volumes. It keeps track of all who try to find it. It takes an individual's blood, sweat and tears through many years to even learn of its existence. And, when this demon finally decides that a select individual is worthy to know that they were, indeed, a contender in this grand eternal fight, it leaves behind a marker. This marker, a relic really, may take years to be found, and then only by someone who has been given the marker before. This burned, rusted, twisted mass of days past, starts out as a treasured piece of our critical equipment. It is taken without our knowledge and transformed on an anvil made up of long hours and late nights, hammered by the blood that was given, twisted by the sweat and tears that were shed and finally formed into the prize that, amongst a small group, brings utter delight. When this marker, this rare relic, is found and given to the one who earned it, if they listen real close to the trees, the grasses and the wind, they may hear the demon speak. It will say, "I am the Truman Lake Fire Demon. I was put here by God to test your mettle, and you have proven yourself a valiant protector of this beautiful land. Be ever vigilant as this struggle will continue, but know that you have earned a respected place in this wonderful, natural world."

Presented to Mike Huffman, November 1, 2014   Josh Shroyer, 2006

Photo of the actual award given to Mike.

What the Truman Lake Fire Demon really looks like.

Chapter 12

The Perfect Backfire

Sometimes, you get lucky

The wind, it was just crazy. Our biggest problem, of many big problems, for the day. We were trying to cut off this fire by using a standard hit the flanks and pinch off the head, but the head was just too intense. Each time the crew got ahead of the fire, Chipper would take the 350 dozer and try to cut a line that would hold the fire. The wind would just blow leaves across the line, there would be too many spotfires to handle, and we would back up, punt and try again. As we were all getting a bit frustrated with this game the fire was playing with us, I called for more resources from dispatch. As it was, the rest of my crew was finishing up on a different fire not far from where we were and was able to respond fairly quickly. Now, at full strength (2 JD 350 fire dozers and 7 people strong), we decided to jump way out in front of the main fire. I instructed both dozers to put in a line that would be 6 blade widths wide. While they were working on that, the rest of us kept the flanks in check and kept steering the beast into the trap we had set for it. With the dozer line done, we all ran back to the newly formed clearing.

I pulled together everyone and gave the instructions and a quick pep talk. "This is where we need to hold this fire. This is where our best chance for success is. We can't afford to lose it again, or we will be fighting from homeowners' backyards. We are running out of time, options, and ground. In addition, there are other fires going on that need our attention, and this fire has overstayed its welcome. It is now or never!" I had a dozer stage at each end of the 400-yard-long line we had just cleared. They would help watch and hold. In addition, we took every drip torch we could muster at the time, which was 4, and I lined myself and 3 others out along the fire line, about 100 yards apart. The last person was in the middle and would watch for spots. Everyone stood, poised and ready for the final run, while the wind just kept howling and pushing the fire towards us really quick. Some were starting to get a bit anxious and wanted to get going with the backfire now. But I held them back and had them wait. I was waiting for the exact right moment. A moment that was not quite here yet. My instincts said to hold true to my plan, but with the way the wind was howling and whipping up the head of the fire, doubts started creeping into my head. "It was not going to work." "What are we doing at the head of this beast?" "Why was my moment not coming?" The fire kept bearing down on us, and then, all of a sudden, I knew we were close.

Then it happened! That slight lull in the wind was the battle for dominance between the main wind and the sucking wind of the fire. I knew this was our one chance. I yelled the order for everyone to tip their drip torches and start setting fire. We ran as hard and as fast as we could, and as everyone made it to the place where the previous person started, we had our backfire set! Within those 20 or 25 seconds, the wind was sucked into the main fire so hard that what we lit was now racing towards the main fire as fast as it was heading to us. As the two fires met, the intensity was ferocious! Fire whirls started spinning up, and then the main wind took over again. We were showered with soot, ash, and hot embers. We were all diligent at watching the green side of the line for any spotfires and were able to jump on the two that started. We worked feverishly to catch both before they could really get established and did so within a few minutes. With those spots contained, we had a brief moment of relief. We looked at each other, and though no words were spoken at that time, we all knew just how lucky we were to have all the ingredients come together at the right combination of time and place to win yet another battle. The main head fire was now gone. Our plan had worked!

We reorganized into 2 crews and could now start attacking the flanks again and get everything tied in. The sun was just setting as we wrapped up this fire and had it mopped up enough to leave it. After that, a quick call to dispatch gave us our new fires to get to and fight, and there we would spend the rest of the night.

While not a photo of the perfect backfire, this is another of many where things went right with moments to spare as I used this 2-track trail to use the backfire to push the main fire into an arm of Truman Lake. Photo by Dan Moran.

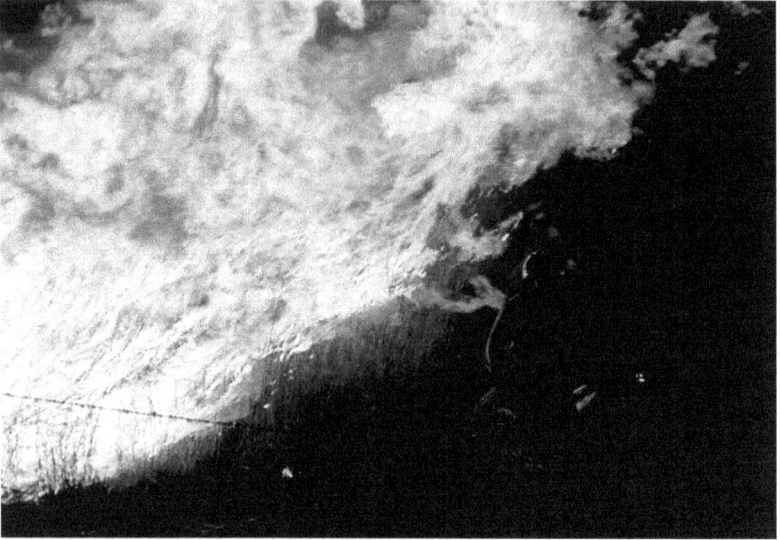

I knew this one was going to be close. I tossed my camera to a crew member
to get some photos and to have documentation if anything
went wrong. Yes, it was close and hot. But we were able to seal
the fire off after this.

Chapter 13

Spike Camp Tables

Doing What We Can for Our Fellow Firefighters

I was on a trip to Idaho, in the Nez Perce NF, as a Felling Boss. The trip started out pretty well, with some good assignments, and I was supervising a colorful pair of fallers. They were as different as different could be. Floyd was a literal grizzly bear of a man. He stood about 6'7", had a full beard, and the Stihl 088 looked like a toy in his huge hands. Dan, on the other hand, was about 5'4", and you were afraid the wind might blow him away at any moment. Floyd would cuss so bad a sailor might blush, while Dan was very quiet and reserved. They both matched each other when it came to cutting and falling trees, however. They worked great together as a team and seemed to know what each other was going to do and complemented each other in how they worked. It was rather fun to watch their interactions with each other, as well as see how other firefighters responded to seeing such a mismatched falling team.

As many details go, we could see that this fire was not going to get us our full 14, so we started looking for ways to get a few extra days. I heard a rumor that they were going to send a number of crews into a spike camp. The problem was, it was on a part of the fire with not much in the way of big trees, well, there were not many trees at all. It was in a big meadow that had burned about 20 years earlier, and there were only scattered snags. Fallers and Felling Bosses were being demobbed like crazy from the fire, so I started campaigning hard. Success came when I met up with an Idaho Department of Lands Forester who was from the local area. Being a state guy myself, I was always on the lookout for other state guys on fire. Since the fire actually started on IDL lands and he was the local IDL contact, he cleared the way for us to get assigned to the spike camp.

While they were going to shuttle the 6 or so crews by helicopter, we had to drive the 5-hour trip up a trail, and I use the term trail loosely. Someone had traveled a game trail and put up flagging to make the way. Keep in mind the game trail we were on seems to have been abandoned by the local game about 10 years earlier. I'm just glad I had a smaller mid-size rental truck to drive. It was easier to weave in and out of the trees that were growing up on the trail. When we finally arrived, it was getting towards evening. My fallers and I decided to just sleep in our trucks and survey our situation in the morning.

As we figured, there was no work for us, so we were told to just hang around the camp. I can hunker with the best of them when needed, but I can't just sit around a camp very well. I chatted with Floyd and Dan, and we came up with a plan in short order. We went to work looking for exactly what we needed, and the guys started up their saws. It took us most of the day to finish our task, as there were only three of us. However, when the crews came back into camp for the evening meal, they were greatly surprised to find their food being served from a table. Once they got their food, they could then sit down at a long row of benches and eat from more tables. We had ripped a bunch of logs that were killed from the previous fire into planks about an inch thick and lashed them to smaller logs to form the tables. For the Benches, we used planks about 2 inches thick. We had provided enough seating for about half of the crew to eat at a time. With well over 100 firefighters in the spike camp, by the time the first ones were served and had eaten, their seats were vacated for the rest of the firefighters to have seats then.

We only had three days in spike camp before we got our demob orders, but those three days were spent in some extraordinarily beautiful country, and we kept ourselves busy helping to make our fellow firefighters more comfortable.

Floyd standing by some of his handiwork.

Floyd, in the orange aluminum hard hat with Dan hidden behind, work
with the Spike Camp Managers use some buckets to support the
middle of the table.

Some additional bench seating under the canopy for a
few more spots to sit.

Chapter 14

Chasing a Bear

What was that Guy Thinking?

Early on in my career, on a fire in Montana as part of a crew. A lot of things were new and exciting, and I was seeig some sights for the first time ever. The fire, in general, was pretty active, and we were also very fortunate to be getting some good assignments. We burned out about 4 miles of line one day. The hotshot crew that was supposed to do the burning never showed up. The Div Sup was not at all happy and wanted the burnout done TODAY! I had used Fuzees before, but the Div Sup showed me how to stack a couple together and then put them on a stick so I wouldn't have to bend over so much. With that new bit of knowledge, I stuck close to him, and he directed me where to light and how much fire to put on the ground. Overall, an awesome day.

Another day, we got to go grid and pick up a bunch of defective "ping pong balls" from an aerial ignition operation that didn't go as planned. They couldn't quite figure out what happened, so they wanted to collect as many of the defective balls as possible so they could study them. We were told we could not keep any, and all had to be turned in. Well, I can neither confirm nor deny that a couple may have become lost in the bottom of my pack and come home with me.

Yet another day, a Task Force Leader got a little ahead of himself on a burn-out operation and allowed a little too much fire to be put on the ground. Of course, this sent everyone into a tizzy. We were told earlier that if something happened, there were 2 safety zones to head to, one uphill and one downhill. We determined that a certain point on the hill would be the breakpoint as to who went up and who went down. When the call came, I was just above the breakpoint, so I had the longest run to the top of the hill. While I was feeling a bit sorry for myself for the long, steep run uphill, I later found out that the part of the crew that went downhill had to keep running as the safety zone they were supposed to use was nothing more than a big grassy meadow. Once the fire hit the grass, it just kept burning and was not a safety zone at all.

Like I said, a pretty active and adventurous fire. Anyway, things had slowed down a bit, and we were spread out doing mop-up. I was working right next to the Crew Boss, and he mentioned that it was time for a break, so as I sat down on a log, he sat next to me. He had worked previously in the KC District, where I had also got my start, so we started talking about what had changed and what had stayed the same. I had pulled out a snack from my pack and had an open canteen of water that I was sipping on.

About that time, a black bear came running by, no more than 15 yards in front of us. I don't think it even knew we were there, or it didn't care, but it paid us no attention and kept going. I, having never seen a bear in person yet, was amazed, and I wanted a picture, so I grabbed my camera from my pack and took off after the bear. At this point, my Crew Boss, thinking I must have lost my mind or something, jumped up and took off after me. He was yelling and shouting at me, but I can't really remember what he was saying. I just wanted to try to catch a glimpse of the bear again so I could snap a photo.

I was feeling pretty confident that I was gaining on the bear, and I felt like a deer, gracefully jumping over downed logs and weaving in and out of small trees that had not completely burned up. Not even the occasional stump hole that caught my boot and tried to trip me up could stop me. By now, my Crew Boss was out of sight behind me, and I could no longer hear him yelling at me.

I finally came to a small clearing and realized I was probably not as fast as I thought I was, as the bear was nowhere to be seen. I did, however, see 2 yellow shirts sitting on a log near the fire line at the far end of the opening. At this point, I figured I would go share my close encounter with them, but something seemed out of place. They both sat statue still. One even had his arm up to his mouth, holding an apple, but still no movement.

As I got about 15 feet from them, I asked if they saw the bear that ran through the area. At the first sound of a voice, they both jumped and hollered at me like I had done something wrong. They go about cussing and yelling at me, both at the same time, and I can't understand what either of them is saying. About this time, my Crew Boss shows up and starts in on me as well.

Finally, everyone settled down enough that we could all speak in reasonable tones. Turns out, the bear did indeed run by them. So close, in fact, that one of them asked, "Did you know a bear's nostrils flare in and out when they breathe?" Wow, that must have been close. About 2 feet, in fact. They said it happened so fast and were frozen with shock, then they heard more movement behind them. They didn't say a word and dared not move an inch as they knew another bear was right behind the first one. Not knowing it was me when I spoke, it jolted them well, as they were not expecting a bear to talk.

It all ended well enough, even if I did give my Crew Boss a scare. He just knew he was going to have to fill out some paperwork for some knuckleheaded rookie getting himself eaten by a bear. By the end of the fire, we were all able to laugh about it. Some more than others. After all, what was that guy thinking?

The Cave Gulch Fire where so many fun things happened. It was later during this fire that I had my first bear encounter.

Chapter 15

I Need a Break

Just Call Danny

This story is about a specific individual that I will call our good luck charm, or maybe we just need to call it "We need a break and need a couple of days off, so we'll call him in," as that's how it always seemed to work anyway. Danny is a good friend and a fellow forester. Early on, we were in the same region, just at different locations. He had since moved on to other parts of the state with different jobs and job titles, but he was always happy to come help when we were in a tight spot, getting short-handed, or having too many fires to deal with.

The way it always seemed to work—we would be having multiple fires, maybe even multiple fires each day. You know, a good five-, six-, or seven-day run, working hard.

Danny would call down and say something like, "Hey, if you need some help, I'll come on down, and I'll bring my crew."

Sure! You know the drill. Come on down, hotel up, and be ready to go first thing in the morning.

Inevitably, he would show up, and we would not have another fire for the next three days. Fire danger was still high, and nothing had really changed—other than no fire calls.

At that point, you figure, well, I guess we can all take a break and go home and catch up on some sleep. So, we'd send Danny and his crew home.

I swear, no sooner than he was back home or in his office, we'd get a fire call. Almost like clockwork.

What is the deal? Did we piss off Big Ernie?

The first couple of times this happened, it was just kind of funny and flabbergasting, and you shook your head. Danny just wanted to come down and truly help out, and they also wanted to gain more experience and work on task books like everyone else. I know it was hard to spend all that time and effort, daring to be away from his family, to come down and not do a thing. Disheartening, in fact. Eventually, it just became a running joke. We'd have a good time calling him up and saying, "Hey, you want to come down? I need a break." He was pretty good at taking the joke, and he accepted the "good luck charm" moniker.

Ultimately, he did make it down and actually helped us fight a few fires. I mean, he's actually a pretty good hand to have and someone who can manage a fire pretty well in and of himself, but it definitely seems like most of the time, he was the one that showed up, and the fires just wouldn't happen. Some say he was living right; some say he was living wrong. Good old Big Ernie. I didn't care. We utilized him in that manner, regardless. I think he even got to where he wouldn't even call, or he would just hear us out on a fire one day, and he just grabbed his crew and showed up. That broke the curse. Well, I mean, it was a curse for him, but we sure wanted the break that he offered. Oh well, at least he was great to have on the fire. Smart, hardworking, and always good for a laugh.

While he did make it on some fires, I think even now, if some parts of the state are having bad fire problems, everyone knows to just call Danny. Send him down, and you'll end up with at least a day break, if not two.

When Danny finally made it on a fire to help out, we just
had to document it!

Chapter 16

Naming Fires

Choose Wisely

Have you ever named a fire? Well, I have once or twice, and believe me, sometimes there is a lot of thought that goes into what to name a fire. Other times, very little thought ends up in the naming. Generally, a fire is named for a local landmark near where the fire starts, whether it be a river, creek, town, draw, ridge, you get the idea. Some notable fires from my career include the Deepwater Fire, Silver Mine Ridge Fire, Salt Creek Fire, White Oak Creek Fire, Highway 18 Fire, Hay Creek Fire, and the Fischbach Ridge Fire.

Sometimes, in our high arson areas, we would have so many fires in a given year that naming became a real challenge. One particular case in point is Dillon Creek. This was an area where the fire bugs hit just about every year, and many times, multiple times a year as well. So, in a particular year in question, we had the Dillon Creek Fire. About 1 week later, we had another fire in the same area, so Dillon Creek 2 Fire. A few days later, Dillon Creek 3 Fire, and so on.

I had some heartburn with just sequentially numbering these fires, as that is what brought about my naming the fires in the first place. Way back in the day, fires were not named unless they were extremely notable. Our agency policy only required numbering the fires. I can remember the old timers talking about a ton of fires, but only a handful actually had names. We usually just named our fires according to our fire report fire numbers. Fires like Fire 178, Fire 183, or Fire 218. Nothing to remember it by or place it in our long-term memory. To this day, I don't remember Fire 476. However, I do remember the Bethel Church Fire. Yes, they were the same fire, and yes, I had to look up the info from my records and notes from long ago.

The Bethel Church Fire was a fire that burned 535 acres from an arson set right next to the old Bethel Church, hence the name. It burned all night, and I never saw the fire in the daylight. I remember this fire due to ribbons of flame stretched out all over the Ozark hills, and we were running down a number of roads assessing threatened structures. If someone had mentioned Fire 476, I would not have remembered all that.

We knew that the Feds (the US Forest Service, BLM, and Park Service) named all their fires. Throughout my career, I have been on some really interesting fires across the country, name-wise, anyway. A few stand out, like the Bucksnort Fire in Montana, Sleepy 91 in Washington, the Blackerby Fire in Idaho, and the Rodeo-Chediski Fire in Arizona. The Pagami Creek Fire in Minnesota, the Ocean Lake Fire in Wyoming, and the State Fire in Utah. Just the name of those fires brings an instant image to mind of what happened there. I wanted the same for all the fires we worked on at home, so I started naming every fire I went on. Again, most were pretty indicative of where they started, Coal Creek Fire, Sapps Landing Fire, B Hwy Fire, Horseshoe Bend Fire, Muddy Creek Fire, and so on.

Soon, with all the arson fires we had, fires started burning over each other, especially year after year. I can go back in my records and see that in one area, we had 12 of 15 years that had at least 1 Bethlehem Fire. In the same year, I had the Davis Quarry

Fire 1 through Davis Quarry Fire 8, as well as Hay Creek Fire 1 through 8. This brings me back to the quandary with the Dillon Creek Fires. So, I started poring over the topo maps, looking for smaller, more obscure place names. I looked at historical maps and asked folks who had been around for a long time if someplace was known by a different name in the past.

I was able to garner a ton of knowledge from the old timers and even found a historical reference to place names of Missouri Counties. This led to coming up with some fairly interesting fire names.

Now, for example, instead of overusing the Deepwater Fire name year after year, so named for Deepwater Creek that ran near the town of Deepwater, I could also name fires White Oak Creek Fire, Marshall Creek Fire, Deepwater Bluff Fire, Deepwater Savanna Fire, Whitacker Lake Fire, Old Hwy 13 North Fire, Old Hwy 13 South Fire, and Railbed Fire. Yes, all actual fires in the Deepwater area.

As I said, naming fires could become difficult at times. In some cases, we were running so hard and fighting so many fires in a row that taking the time to look at a map to see what cool name you could come up with was not a priority. This led to some rather boring fire names. There was the Rabbit Fire due to the only thing that separated that fire from all the others that week was the vast number of rabbits running around. There was a fire on an unnamed, unnumbered road that burned a log cabin to the ground. I called it the Log Cabin Fire. I had a Dead-End Fire at the end of a dead-end road. The Thanksgiving Fire occurred on, wait for it, you guessed it, Thanksgiving. I named the Osage Fire for a variety of native switchgrass that was burning. The Fence Fire was so named because of the large amount of fence burned, and that was damaged. We even all agreed to call one fire, the Shots Fired Fire, since the excitement for the night was shots being fired.

Some other real creative fires I am responsible for naming include the Baler Fire, caused by a hay baler catching fire and burning hundreds of acres of hay and grass. The Cove Fire, located at the back end of a cove, and of course, the Lightning Fire. This was a lightning-caused fire that I had to turn over to one of my crew as I was leaving to head to Washington the next day for a fire detail. He asked what to call it, and, well, I had nothing better to offer.

Speaking of some real genius fire names. We had a run of fires that we just called for what was the cause of the fire. Like the Baler Fire and Lightning Fire mentioned above, we also had the Car Fire, started from a stolen, torched car, the Truck Fire, and the ATV Fire. We fought the House Fire, which started as a house fire and then burned over 100 acres on a windy day, the Shed Fire, and the Trash Fire, which started from a trash barrel. Finally, there was the Powerline Fire during a windstorm, the Fireworks Fire on the 4th of July, and one fall during hunting season, the Hunter Fire.

These days, there a protocols, rules, and restrictions to naming fires. With everyone trying to be so politically correct, we don't want to take a chance of offending anyone. We can't name fires for the private property they are on. So, previous fires I had, like the Magnum Fire, Arduzer Fire, and Fisher Fire, would not work in today's environment. One might also need to consider who they might offend. I guess by having a Tightwad Fire, I could offend some tightwad somewhere. However, those who live in the community of Tightwad might be proud to have a fire named after them. See, there is even a bank in that town, and folks come from all over the country to open an account in the Tightwad Bank. Sadly, as of this publishing, the Tightwad Bank is no longer in business. Would I offend the French with my French Bridge Fire? Poor Granny might take issue with the Granny's Acres Fire.

The local coon hunters might feel left out if I only used the Fox Hunter's Fire. I would not want to discriminate, so I have both the Trailer Park Fire and the Country Club Fire. Also, don't lose sight of the Gouge Eye Fire. Finally, don't let the Thrush Fire leave a bad taste in your mouth.

In thinking back on all the fires I have ever named, some just sound different and may create a different image than what was reality. Take, for example, the Silver Creek Fire. While it sounds beautiful, it was really a dirty creek and a fire I would rather forget. Then there was the Forbes Fire, but I don't recall getting rich or famous on that one. The Dam Pond Fire, no, I am not cussing that fire; there really is a pond called Dam Pond, and that is where the fire started. The Flat Prairie Fire was mostly flat but did have some terrain to deal with. Was the False Fire really a fire?

Some fires, on the other hand, create a pretty good picture of what we saw. To start with, take the Homemade Bomb Fire. That is the most memorable part of that fire, finding an undetonated homemade bomb. We think it malfunctioned and actually caused the fire. There was the Blow Down Fire, burning a bunch of blow-downs from a 95-mile-per-hour derecho. The Red Rock fire was so named for all the red rock in the area, and the Lagoons Fire occurred around the lagoons. Finally, I will offer the Single Pile Fire, where all that burned was a single pile of illegally dumped leaves and yard debris.

I can't help but also think back to some other memorable fires just due to the fact of having good memories of co-workers, awesome firefights, seeing the sunrise come up, or any of a bunch of other good memories. Fires like the White Rock Fire burned thousands of acres and really challenged our tactics. The Shockman Fire burned just over 400 acres, but I think I walked about 15 miles around it that night. The Valhalla Fire was in a very remote area that burned over 1,000 acres and took 3 days to contain. Or, the Younger Fire, where we were able to just sit back and work together as a crew and not worry about the pressures of structures or mutual aid.

Then there are the fires with not-so-pleasant memories. The White Oak Fire, where a firefighter went down. The Deepwater Fire (one of many called the Deepwater Fire), where there was an entrapment, as well as the Hwy 18 Fire, which also had 2 entrapments. The B&E Complex Fires, where a large number of homes were lost, or the B&M Fire, which would be the last fire for one of my good friends and mentors. Then there was another Shockman Fire that, due to some very poor upper management, almost caused me to walk away from the fire service for good. Thankfully, a long weekend with my family to decompress led to a more level-headed decision.

I could go on and on about the hundreds and hundreds of fires I have named over the years, but I think I will switch and talk about fires that others have named. Some of those fires, I have no idea why they were called what they were called. Some of this has to do with rules these days of having a fire named before aircraft can be ordered up. So, even before the first on-the-ground firefighter has arrived, the fire has been named by someone looking at a map who is a couple of hours away from where the fire is and jots down a name. A few that come to mind that happened this way include the Bull Canyon Fire, located not in Bull Canyon but three canyons over in Dry Gulch. Or the South Fork 1 Fire, which was actually north of the North Fork drainage. Then there was the Red Lakes Fire that was nowhere near the Red Lakes Subdivision, or the Buffalo Fire that was over 10 miles from Buffalo Creek, and I think it should have been called the Copper Mountain Fire since it was within walking distance of the top of Copper Mountain.

Then, there are other fires I have heard about or read about. Take the Speedy Turtle Fire. Makes you wonder how they came up with that one. Or the Fancy Fire. Did they have to wear ties with their Nomex? Or, what kind of setting was the Tranquil Fire burning in?

I miss naming fires as I am not as involved in the initial attack as I used to be. There were some fire names I never got to use. I waited for a long time to have a Wolf Creek Fire, but there was never a fire in that drainage. I also never got around to using the Bad Luck Fire or the Sun Up Fire, even though I saw a number of fires where the sun came back up. I am glad I will never again have to have a Deepwater Fire or a Dillon Creek Fire. I would have liked to have had one more Silver Mine Ridge Fire with my old mentors, or better yet, to sit down with them and name some of the old numbered fires we fought together and see what names we could have come up with. That would have been priceless. I can only use my imagination at this point, as I will never have that opportunity now.

Now, later in my career, there are some memorable fires that have special memories. These are mostly due to the team I was on or the teammates I worked with. Even moving into a Liaison Officer role and not directly tied to suppression efforts, fire names keep the memory banks fresh. There was the Lava Mountain Fire, where I didn't actually fight any flames, but as an Agency Rep, fought the politics of fire, and the Sugarloaf Fire, where I helped smooth over the politics of Federal versus private land politics. There was the Calwood Fire, where I had to have a "discussion" with a local Sheriff and explain that, yes, he was indeed in charge of the public evacuation; we could only recommend. There was the Pedro Mountain Fire and the Chris Mountain Fire, where I was able to work alongside my wife. There was the Mullen Fire that challenged every person on the fire every day.

I will leave you with a few remaining fire names, but I won't offer any background to them. They have meaning to me and those who were there at the time. I will just let your imagination run with them. There was the Bean Breeder Fire, the Spangler Fire, the Maggard Wixted Fire, the WahKanTah Fire, and the Cooper Creek Fire. The Otter Creek Fire, the Brownington Point Fire, the Lincoln Fire, and the Mule Shoe Fire. There was the 64 Road Complex, one of many Galliniper Creek Fires, the D Road Fire, the Grand River Fire, and finally, Fire #374. Rest in Peace, ML.

The D Road Fire. Yep, D Road was where it started.

Chapter 17

The Unique Smell of Smoke

Can't Hide Anything

Smoke smells like smoke, right? It is unpleasant, burns the throat, waters the eyes, and seems to follow you no matter where you sit around a campfire. I never put much more thought into it than that. I think, under the surface, deep down, I knew there was a drastic difference, but it really never came up in discussion.

Some of our fire seasons were full of weeks on end of daily fires. Depending on the time of year, different things would burn. If we went into a drought, we could have fires go right from our "normal" late winter/early spring season into summer. A second "season" in the fall happens most years, as well as leaves turning colors, eventually turning brown and falling. Without snow cover, we could move right into the dead of winter.

In our fire coverage area, we had fires burn in all manner of fuels. We had tall native grasses in our prairies and glades, short grass that was mainly fescue, leaf litter that was either oak and hickory, or in other places, made up of many other species like maple, ash, cottonwood, and sycamore. We had old fields that were made up of cedar (juniper) briars and thorny brush. There were fields of invasive serecia lespedeza, and then there was the flood zone of Truman Lake, where thousands of acres of bottomland hardwoods had been killed due to the flooding and were now a mix of dead trees, both standing and fallen over, mixed with annual weeds like ragweed.

Early on, you started realizing that some fuels were not as "fun" to have burning, while others were not so bad. Native grasses like we had on the prairies and glades were some of the best, relatively speaking. Other than a slight burnt tinge, the smoke actually smelled natural and earthy. On the other end of the spectrum was green fescue smoke. When the fescue was turning green in the spring but still had enough dead thatch to keep the fire burning, this smoke was thick. Thick and nasty, and instantly made your eyes sting and water. Your lungs screamed, and your mouth and nose revolted.

Being a man of few words, when my wife, Tammy, would ask how the fire was, I would usually give short answers like, "Not too bad," or "We had three today," or maybe, "It was a butt-kicker due to the wind." But I never got into too many details.

Well, as you can surmise, this was not good enough for my wife, who had fought fires beside me and knows what we deal with better than most. She turned it on me one day. I'm sure I said something like, "Not too bad," to the question and then stopped. She said, "You were in the bottoms again."

"Yeah… how did you know?"

But I didn't want to get too deep into it.

A day or two later, she didn't even ask; she just stated, "The fescue is greening up pretty good."

Ok, now I'm intrigued. How is she getting this information? I mean, I usually would tell her a general location of where I was, and sometimes specific locations, but never that detailed. Turns out, she was making all the mental notes studying the information I gave her and comparing it with her nose. And, truth be told, she became pretty dang good at it.

This led to some informal categorizations of smoke. While I don't think we ever had a "good" smoke, there were some that were better than others. Definitely some bad smokes. The bad smokes were fescue, the bottoms, and any that involved manmade materials. We always tried to stay out of the smoke if houses or cabins burned, but it was not always possible. Some of the unique smokes were the native grasses of the prairies. Smoke from cedar or juniper would fall into this category, as would any time a pine was burning. Oak leaves migrated between ok and bad, depending on the time of year and whether there was moisture on the bottom layer of leaves. The wetter the leaves, the more towards bad it became.

While words will never really be able to accurately describe each smoke, if you have smelled enough different kinds of smoke enough times, you can start to differentiate. Even now, if we are driving through an area where smoke is hanging low, Tammy will perk up and randomly throw out comments like "wet oak leaves," "someone is burning their prairie," or "I wonder if that was a trash pile or someone's home."

Regardless, I learned early on that I had better fess up on what was going on and where I had been, as the smoke smell stuck to my fire clothes would tell on me. I can't hide anything.

Sunset after a long day.

Another smoke smell that is hard to deal with is when hay
burns during some of these fires.

Chapter 18

The Younger Fire

Just a Good Ol Fire

Every now and then, we had to fight a fire with just our small group. We would not be coordinating multiple agencies or have structures threatened. We would just be out in a remote area by ourselves. What would end up being called the Younger Fire turned out to be just that fire in March of 2014. As it was, I did have an FWS employee with me for the day as he was working on an ICT5 Task Book. Earlier, we did get on a small wind-driven fire in short grass, but that was not really a good training fire in my mind, even though it did qualify as a Type 5 fire.

Early afternoon, our detection plane called in a fire that I knew immediately would be a good training fire for my trainee. It was in a fairly remote area of St. Clair County, and took a bit to drive even close to the fire. As we arrived, I told Chris that this would be his fire and I would observe. Chris was more than ready, and he took care of talking with Dispatch in short order and getting extra resources ordered. Since the next arriving resources were still at least 30 minutes out, we decided to hike into the fire and get a better size-up.

A short 3/4-mile hike, and we got to the fire. It was burning with a number of heads, and luckily, they were headed into Truman Lake, so at least we were not going to have to chase this one.

The terrain was easy to moderate, with some areas of exposed rock. The entire area was a typical woodland as is found in West Central Missouri. It was even more so due to the fact that this area seems to burn about every 3 or so years when the local fire-bugs torch it off. Of course, by the time we get there, they are long gone and probably boozed up back wherever home may be.

We hiked enough of the fire to get a good initial plan for how to deploy our incoming resources, which included one of our fire doz-ers, a UTV, and 5 fellow firefighters. Since the fire was spread out over a couple of ridges, Chris and I worked out that he would stay in command of the fire and direct the suppression while I went ahead and scouted the fire farther to the north. The plan was to anchor and flank with the dozer line and burn out as needed. Even though the wind was starting to die down, we were starting to get terrain-driven fire in up-slope runs only to hit the ridge and then be wind-driven in a different direction. Not long after I left on my scouting mission, our resources started arriving, and I listened as Chris directed them to the anchor point. There, he met up with them and, laid out the suppression strategy, and gave the safety briefing.

I felt comfortable leaving Chris to figure some things out without me standing right on his hip the entire time. As all of the incoming resources were either from my own staff or fellow employees with whom we work all the time, I knew they would also be helping to make sure Chris did not make any big errors. This gave me time to get to the north end of the fire and get a good idea of the overall fire picture. I radioed Chris with my information and informed him I was headed back to the initial anchor spot. On my way back, I started hearing radio traffic on our tactical channel about the fire bumping the dozer line pretty hard. Then there was a small break-over. I knew from the tone of the voices of "My" guys that there was nothing to worry about, and I figured out this was just a good learning opportunity for my trainee. I won't go into all the radio traffic and maneuvering; I will just relate what happened.

As with many trainees, it is easy to get caught up in all the new responsibilities that some of the basics get forgotten. I will include myself in this as I can remember when I was new and working with guys who had been doing this a lot longer than I had. Anyway, my dozer operator was following directions from Chris as to where to put the line. Knowing that the line placement on the fire side of the ridge was not the best spot, but also recognizing that the worst that could happen, given the day, was to lose the line and put the line in the correct placement on the lee side of the ridge, he forged ahead. Of course, with the terrain-driven fire, the dozer line got bumped pretty hard, and the slop-over resulted. As I caught up with Chris, I could tell he already knew what had happened and how to fix the problem. He had redirected the dozer to the blade line on the lee side of the ridge, and when we started burning out from the line, of course, the fire ran uphill to the ridge and met with the main fire, and everyone was a lot cooler and breathing less smoke. Well, being his trainer for the day, we talked about this. He felt bad about missing a very basic suppression tactic, but as I told him, by making this mistake and getting the chance to fix it right, he would not make that mistake again, and he would also be more apt to remember the basics next time. I have come to realize that no matter how many times we get things driven into our heads until we actually see things play out and sometimes make some mistakes, we have trouble solidifying the lesson learned. As I stated earlier, everyone on the fire was watching out for the trainee and knew how to keep themselves and Chris safe while letting him learn this valuable lesson.

With the terrain-driven fire wanting to keep making uphill runs, we figured the best way to get around this fire was to keep up on the ridges. We knew from previous fires in the area that an old road went down a main ridge running from South to North. This allowed us to stay ahead of the upslope runs and continue to burn out, running our burnout with the wind behind us into the upslope moving main fire. We finally came to a known trail on the North side of the fire that wound back down to the lake, and we knew as soon as we burned that out we had this fire contained. I bounced back and forth with Chris, making sure I was available to answer any questions he may have and spotting and flagging snags that the dozer could push on its way out.

Once the fire was tied in and the entire line was burned out, we started working our way back to the trucks, checking the line and dealing with snags on the way. Earlier, when I had some cell phone signal on the highest ridge, I made a call to the National Weather Service (NWS), in Springfield. From that call, I learned that humidity recovery overnight was not going to be great, and we were to expect a wind shift from SW to NE by daybreak. We made sure to mop up the SW portion of the fire line, anticipating this wind shift. It was well past dark by the time we all made it to the vehicles. I held a quick AAR, or After Action Review, to discuss the day. Everyone offered good and constructive comments, and Chris thanked everyone for helping him with his trainee fire. He could tell he was working with a group of firefighters who really knew what they were doing but also went out of their way to help him as he tackled the responsibility of becoming an initial attack IC.

I spent a little more time talking with Chris after everyone left, and he and another firefighter would come back in the morning and walk the line again and continue mop-up to be sure the fire was truly out. All told, the fire burned 320 acres and took about 7 hours to contain with the 7 of us on the scene. It was a good training fire for me to train a new IC and a good fire for us to just sit back and do what we are trained to do without the headaches of multi-agency coordination, structures threatened, worrying about closing a road, or many other issues. If only all our fires could be this fun and easy.

Finally getting around the head of the fire enough to cleanup and burn out from the trail.

Once this all burned out, the fire goes into mop-up mode.

Chapter 19

Cutting Trees

I May Have Cut One or Two

There are one or two snags in the area where I spent a lot of my career, specifically West Central Missouri in the Truman Lake area. First, you need to understand Truman Lake was designed and built by the US Army Corps of Engineers as a flood control project to help keep the lower Missouri River from flooding. By doing so, the normal flood control pool encompassed what was once home to vast acres of bottomland hardwood forests. The repeated floods eventually drowned out and killed all these forests, leaving hundreds of thousands, if not millions, of snags. I never really took the time to count them, so you will just have to take my word for that. It's a fact!

In some years, when the lake level would stay down, that flood-killed timber would start growing a huge crop of annual weeds that was the perfect fuel for all the arsonists in the area to go light off. But with all the dead-standing snags, it also meant a huge problem not only from a safety standpoint but a control standpoint. Once a snag caught fire and started blowing embers into the unburned fuel, we were off to the races again. For this reason, we cut a lot of snags in that area.

Our normal operations seemed to be to fight the fire and try to stop its forward progress during the day and then mop up and cut snags at night. Wait. What? Yes, you heard that right. We cut snags at night. A. Lot. Of. Snags. At. Night.

A lot of things have changed over the years, and somebody new to the Sawyer or Faller world might question our tactics and what we did back then. That is fine. You need to understand it was a different time and, maybe, a different place. The agency just wanted the fires out. We just wanted to be done so we could go back home. If we waited until morning light to start cutting snags, inevitably, spotfires would pop up, and all the efforts from the previous day were for naught. We were always shorthanded, and all effort was put into stopping the fire spread. Only when we caught the fire due to the wind laying down in the evening could we get into mop up and snagging. This kind of became the daily, or should I say, nightly routine for many of our fire seasons when "the bottoms," as we called them, burned.

Would I cut a snag at night now? Um, well, no, probably not. Can it be done safely? Maybe. We did what we did out of necessity. Keep in mind these were flat lands, with no terrain involved. It was kind of like walking across a moonscape. Once all the fine fuels burned off, there wasn't much left except the snags. Previous fires or floods either burned up or carried away most of the larger fuel that had already fallen.

This was such an issue for us from a fire control standpoint that even outside of fire season, we started cutting swaths through the snag patches. When a wildfire got started, we would try to corral the fire into one of these pre-cut areas so we wouldn't have to cut so much at night. Another interesting thing was as the trees were either rotting and falling down, getting burned up, or were cut by us, the overall number of snags started getting fewer and fewer, at least in our high-fire areas. In this regard, we actually began to feel safer with our nighttime cutting operations. There were fewer snags, and they were starting to get spaced farther apart, so the risk of a domino effect went down with time.

For those who haven't cut hardwood snags, you are missing out. You should really give it a try. Pin oak, a typical bottomland hardwood in the area, was very tall and straight. They had a tendency to hold their lower limbs, which could make for an interesting time getting into the trunk to cut. Others, after all the main limbs had either fallen or had burned up, left you with a tall pole. No weight in the top makes for an interesting falling job. Add to that, once the wood cures and dries, it can become extremely hard. One tree in particular was one of these old pin oak snags, about 28 inches in diameter and still reaching about 75 feet in the air. Put in a typical face cut and get your back cut, and the tree just sits there. Well, we can always wedge it over, right? Remember, it is dark. All we have is our feeble headlamp, and now we are going to start pounding on this dead tree with a brittle top? Right, not a good situation. Luckily, we were able to shine a couple headlights up to the top and just make sure we didn't pound in any sort of cadence that may have rattled something loose. We eventually got it down.

Speaking of hard. Has anyone cut a hedge tree? Also known as Osage Orange, it is one of the densest woods in North America. It is on par with the desert ironwood from the Southwest. Even green it can be rough on your saw chain. Once dead and dried? Sparks fly. One other thing to consider is when this wood burns, it burns hot and pops with a lot of sparks and embers. So, cutting one of these burning snags was always a treat. So much so that we fought over who got to go cut it! Ah, those were the days.

Another interesting snag I cut in those bottomlands was a huge sycamore. I really don't even know how it was still standing. It was over 6 feet in diameter and had a huge cat face or place where it had previously burned and was hollow throughout. It still had a number of large main branches that had not fallen or broken out. Lucky for me, this was not a night operation. However, it was about to fall over a gravel road, so it took a bit of thought and finesse to get it down where I wanted it to go.

Over the years, I have had the opportunity to cut trees and snags across many states. Most of this was due to firefighting efforts, but some were hazardous or high-risk trees near some critical infrastructure. What I have come to understand, for me anyway, is I prefer to cut conifers over hardwood trees any day, or night for that matter. Falling trees is very science-based. You just need a basic understanding of mechanics and to be very good at judging a tree.

A classic example of this is a 12-inch diameter lodgepole pine that was right next to a cabin in the mountains of Wyoming. By right next to, I mean within about 4 feet from the window, and the cabin owner was concerned about his cabin. There should be good reason for this concern as well. The tree should have been cut when the cabin was built, but they thought they wanted it for whatever reason. Roots were cut when installing the cabin's foundation, and on top of that, the tree leaned over the house. Long story a bit shorter, I agreed to cut the tree and mitigate the risk to the cabin.

The tree measured 12 inches in diameter, and I measured it at 100 feet tall. I also estimated that with the lean, the center of gravity was a 12-foot back lean. Now, the simple explanation is that we need to move the center of gravity back over the center and then to the non-cabin side of the tree. If I can put the face cut and back cut in and use a couple wedges, I can "lift" the tree. So, if I can lift the tree 1.44 inches here at the base, where my back cut is, I have now put the center of gravity dead center. A little more, and I can fall the tree away from the cabin. Stacking two wedges will give me plenty of lift. Ultimately, the tree went where we wanted it to, the cabin owner was happy, and I made a few bucks.

This brings me back to conifers and hardwoods. I just feel that the taller, straight trees are a lot easier to judge and measure and get your numbers. Once you have those numbers, it is just mechanics, and you can put most trees where you want them. Short, wide-crowned trees, like many hardwood species, present so many more variables. The inputs are still the same, however, judging the center of gravity on a 45-foot-tall tree that has a crown spread of 45 feet with a trunk that starts out at 18 inches. However, this trunk has a severe "lean" to one side, but the majority of the branches and leaves are on the other side. The reality of this tree is that if you misjudge the center of gravity and are trying to correct a back lean, being off by as little as 2 feet can spell disaster. Trust me. The math works. Mechanics are mechanics. Oh, and you must know the wood qualities of the species you are cutting, as well as wind speed and direction, your altitude, the soundness of the wood fibers, and whether the tree is alive, recently dead, or long dead. But all that could be its own separate book.

To wrap this up, I prefer to cut conifer over hardwoods and taller trees over shorter trees. Diameter does not matter to me, but tree species sometimes matter. So, while I don't cut many trees these days, yeah, in the past, I may have cut one or two.

Me cutting a nice cat-faced oak right on the fireline
that had caught fire.

Some of the snags posed some real safety concerns.

Another of many dead snags that caught fire and had to be cut down.

Some areas were full of dead burning snags.

Chapter 20

Nicknames

How I Got Mine

Early on in my career, I ended up with a great group of older firefighters. These guys would go on to become some of the best mentors I could ever have asked for. They taught me so much about fire but also about life, nature, and teamwork. While I have been part of a lot of teams in my long career, I dare say that this particular group may have demonstrated the best definition of "team," I think there is. What was it, you ask? Sadly, I don't think I can define it well enough to do them justice. There was so much mutual respect. Respect that transcended friendships as well as titles. Knowing that each had the other's back, no matter what. There was the knowing what each other was thinking and a lot of "unspoken" communication.

The thing I noticed about this group was I had to look in the employee files to know what their actual names were, as they all had nicknames. Everybody called them by those nicknames, even the higher-ups from the head shed, so to speak. If you have gotten to this point in the book, you have run across names like Dynamite, GT, Chipper, and Flash. But there was also Crazy Eddie, Monte, Red, and others. As the new kid on the block, I didn't ask about it. I just called them by what everyone else called them. I also noticed that there were others outside of the team that didn't have nicknames. This really made me wonder. Did they just not like using a nickname? Had one not been bestowed? Why was there this dichotomy?

As it was, I was the new Forester who was "supervising" this group. Actually, it was 2 different teams, or Work Teams, as they were called, and worked out of 2 different locations. While they worked on their own separate areas and projects about half the time, they also worked together the other half of the time. I used supervising in quotations above, and I was their supervisor on paper. I had the task of rating their performance, setting work team goals, and managing the budget. But the reality was they were supervising me. Making sure the new kid didn't do something stupid and teaching me the ways of working together. To this day, I only use the term Supervisor as that is what the agency said I had to use. I prefer to think of all this differently. To me, they were my mentors, co-workers, pseudo-father figures, and teachers. To us collectively, we were a team, a crew. It wasn't my crew or my team; it was our crew, our team, and as such, I felt included from day one.

I showed up at this work location in the middle of the fire season. In fact, half the crew I first met along a fire line in the middle of nowhere. This was before even the first phone call or talking on the radio. There was work to be done, and we got to it. This went on for the first few weeks, stretching into months; fight fires, work the public areas we had charge of, and do forest inventory and chainsaw thinning projects. The team was firing on all cylinders.

Fast forward about six months into the job. I called over to the other shop location—I needed to talk with my tech, Dynamite, about some budget items that didn't get funded.

GT answered the phone. I said hello, asked how things were going—all that sort of stuff. Then I asked if Dynamite was around.

He hollered across the shop, "Torch is on the phone for you!"

Shortly after, Dynamite got on the line, and we discussed what we needed to discuss. As we were about to end the call, I asked him about the "Torch" comment.

I heard him chuckle. He played it off, then added, "Come on over in the morning—we could use your help on a project."

The next morning, I drove the 45 minutes to their shop location. I park and go into the open bay door, and there I see both teams sitting in chairs lined up in a semi-circle, with a single chair out in front. Oh boy, this does not look good. What happened? Did I fail at my job? Did I say something wrong? Dynamite and Chipper, the 2 Techs from each work team, both said to have a seat. I have a seat. They are all looking serious. Dynamite says I need to ask the question from yesterday in front of the whole group. At this point, my mind is racing! What question? What is going on? I've never (at least in the 6 months I have known them) seen these guys so serious. They were usually smiling, cutting up, and making jokes.

They had me totally flustered. I stammered a bit, visibly uncomfortable. I don't really remember if I was able to say anything or just stumble over words, but after what seemed an eternity, they all just busted out laughing. At this point, they explain what is happening. I was one of the few who was immediately accepted into their ranks, literally from day one. They had bestowed my nickname that first day. Remember the fire I mentioned earlier about meeting half the crew for the first time on a fire line? Yeah, that one. I was dragging a drip torch along, firing out the dozer line, when I met GT for the first time ever. He is the one who gave me my nickname. Said he wondered who the heck this new "boss" was and was he worth anything. He went on to explain that seeing me walk up, the fire raging behind me, wincing from the heat a bit, but doing what I needed to do to keep the burning line going and greeting him with a smile, he knew I was ok. After I left the fire that evening, and they were all loading up before they headed back to their shop, they had a quick discussion about me and my first impressions. From that point forward, I was known as Torch to each of them.

The funny thing, they used my new nickname all the time, but I guess I didn't hear it or know the right context or something. They all thought it was kind of funny that it took me 6 months to figure it out.

As far as others who came to the crew over the years, I will share a few of their nicknames and the stories behind them. First, there was AAA, as in "triple-A," due to this person having a huge tendency to get trucks stuck. I'll only give away a little hint of who it was, other than we could always tell in her voice over the radio that she was stuck again and was going to need some help. Some of these stuck trucks required the use of the dozers to get her out. In looking back over her career, I think this is the only "downside" she ever had. She was hard-working, willing to do anything that was asked, super intelligent, quick with a funny joke, and didn't take herself too seriously, all wonderful qualities that she still has to this day. Although, I don't think she gets stuck near as much anymore.

There was Sparky. He was so eager to learn as a new forester and was totally eaten up with the firefighting part of the job. You hear the term "sparkplug" for people who get other people excited about doing something. Sparky was that guy. He was destined to do great things and was a natural leader. While his fire career took a different direction, his forestry career is at the top, where, without saying too much, he is heading up a prominent state forestry program in his home state with his wonderful family, doing great things. I have no doubt he is still a sparkplug and still deserving of the name Sparky.

Finally, we have DK. DK could stand for a number of things. Those of a certain age may remember the video game Donkey Kong, and before the texting shortcuts of IDK, there was just Don't Know in our everyday speak. But for one of our crew members, a kid really, this stood for Dumb Kid. He was a great worker, hard worker really, but he also did things that a young kid might do. He took it well, and we all kind of knew it was a short-term name he would have to endure. Chipper was the one who bestowed this nickname, and he even admitted that DK was growing out of the name and said he would remove it as soon as DK earned a new name. Sadly, Chipper passed away before that could happen, so we collectively removed that nickname from the rolls. No longer a kid, he ended up moving into the position that Chipper had held and had performed that job duty well in his long career. I'm certain Chipper would be proud of who DK turned out to be.

To close this chapter out, I go back to how much this group of people meant to me. Probably the best team I have ever been on. You had to earn your nickname, but once you earned it, you were a part of them. I miss that group of guys greatly. So many parts of who I am today can be tied back to them in some way, shape, or form. So many great memories from so many great mentors, co-workers, teammates, and, yes, friends.

Yes, I have a propensity for dragging the drip torch.

Here I am burning out on a section of the White Oak Creek Fire.
Photo by Dan Moran.

Chapter 21

Flying Fire Patrol

Stomach of Steel

Almost immediately after I got to my workstation in Clinton, I found out that flying fire patrol was a part of the job. Now, this was a wonderful realization as I have had a fascination with flying since I was a small child. I got my first taste of flying in a single-engine plane when I was about 6 or 7, I think. My dad was a Shop Teacher, and one of his former students was a pilot and took us up in his plane for a ride, and I was hooked. I don't really remember much about the flight other than I just enjoyed being able to look down on everything.

Fast forward many years, and I figured I wanted to finally learn to fly. A friend of my wife was a pilot, and, bonus, he taught flying lessons! Being that we had only been married about a year and a half and Tammy was in an unpaid internship, it was all we could do to scrape together money for each lesson. Now, if I told you these lessons were out of a small-town airport with not much going on, I would be lying. In fact, these lessons were out of the Kansas City Downtown airport, so it was fairly busy with planes and helicopters of all sizes coming in and out at a fairly frequent pace.

To be honest, this was a bit intimidating for me. I was hoping to be pretty relaxed on my first lesson, but no, here I was, in line with what seemed like 100 passenger jets, private corporate jets, and other small, single-engine planes. My instructor talked me through it all, and as the moment of truth came, I throttled up and released the brakes, and down the runway we went. A pull of the yoke and we lifted off and gained altitude. It was wonderful to be in the air. We took a few laps around the bottoms of Kansas City, took in the skyline to our South, and then headed back for my first landing. Well, due to a pretty good crosswind, my instructor took us in for my "first" landing.

I took a handful more lessons, but unfortunately, I never did complete my training and, therefore, never got my pilot's license. In some regards, I have a little regret about that, but then, on the other hand, that would have just been yet another expensive hobby for me to dump money into.

Anyway, back to Clinton. As we phased out the fire towers and relied more on aerial detection of fires, we utilized both agency planes and agency pilots as well as contract pilots. I have to say, I did prefer flying with the agency guys better, but I will get to them in a bit. I want to start out with one of our contract pilots, who I will call CJ. CJ lived in Osceola and had been flying for quite some time. I can't remember if I ever knew how old he was, but I would guess late 60's or even early 70's. Most of the time, I would just drive to the Osceola airport and meet CJ, and we would fly from there to do our rounds of the region.

One day, I got a call from the Regional Forester asking if I could go up with CJ to do a quick lap of the region. We really hadn't planned on flying that day, but the night before, the local fire bugs really went to town in the central part of the region, and he wanted a quick look to see if we found all the fires. Since this was a last-minute thing, I called and just asked CJ to pick me up at the Clinton airport as I was a bit busy, and it would save me the time of driving to him. No problem. He would meet me in a bit.

I don't really remember much of the flight or of any fires we spotted that day, but what I do remember is our final landing. I had flown with our agency pilots in and out of Clinton Airport many times and kind of had the flight path memorized. As we finish our final turn and get lined up with the runway, I feel like something is not quite right. Not wanting to be "that guy," I don't say anything. However, as we get closer to the runway and lower to the ground, my fears are starting to be confirmed. We are well below the normal glide path, and I don't think we are going to even make it to the runway. I holler at CJ over the noise of the engine, expressing my concern. Nah, he is fine; he has flown into this airport many times, he assures me. This, unfortunately, does not assure me. I mentioned that we have the whole runway and can level out just a bit, but to no avail. Besides, time is up anyway. We are about on the ground, and the runway is still a ways in front of us. I brace for impact.

Overall, the landing was not as rough as I had expected, although it was rough enough. We just barely made the runway, and I do mean just barely. I think we actually hit the lip of the concrete with the tires and bounced a bit, but CJ regained control and finally landed. I was fine, other than some choice words in my mind that this was the absolute last time I was flying with CJ. As we taxied up to the drop-off point, I asked if CJ was going to shut down and hit the restroom before heading back to Osceola. He was kind of short with me and just said no, he was just going to get going. Funny, I thought, my bladder was ready for some relief, but oh well, I can take care of my bladder, he can take care of his, and his flight should only be about 15 minutes anyway.

I wasn't able to talk with the Regional Forester for a couple days due to fires keeping us busy in different parts of the region. When I did, I mentioned what had happened and said I would not be flying with CJ again. He then proceeded to tell me that I wouldn't have to worry. Turns out, the landing was actually pretty rough for poor old CJ. When we landed, we did hit the lip of the runway, and in the resulting jolt, CJ broke his foot and lower leg. He was able to take off and land again in Osceola but wasn't able to walk to his truck. He decided on his own that he was probably done flying and to be honest, I don't think he ever did again. Talking with others who knew CJ, that landing shook him up pretty good, and he was pretty embarrassed about the whole ordeal.

After losing that contract pilot, we were pretty much at the mercy of the agency pilots from then on. Being that we were arguably the hottest region when it came to fire suppression, we didn't really have much to worry about and generally got a plane whenever we wanted or needed one. We had some good fire pilots, and we had some great fire pilots. One, who I will call CH, was ex-military and had spent more hours in aircraft than I could imagine. He not only flew the planes but also our helicopter. CH was a joy to fly with, and, really, we didn't need to send anyone up with him to begin with. He was excellent at spotting fires and giving all the info needed to the ground resources. However, I think he liked the company, and I liked flying with him, so we made it work.

Now, I never did get a full download of what kind of aircraft CH flew in the military or where, but to fly with him, you knew he felt very comfortable with flying. We would spot a fire, and he would turn into a tight circle, putting me directly over the fire so I could give the size up to Dispatch or the resources on the ground once they got on the scene. He would just continue the tight circles until it was time to fly to the next smoke. Looking out the side of the plane, straight down, looking at the map, and talking on the radio made for some equilibrium problems for me. Basically, I got dizzy and lost my horizon. Many times, I would have to ask CH to level off so I could get my bearings fixed. Once, I think he was messing with me and just rolled onto the other side, so he was looking down at the fire like he would do if he was flying alone. This just made things worse for me, as now all I can see is the blue sky out my window. If I looked forward, my horizon was all messed up. I finally told him, "CH, I have never puked in your plane, and I don't want this to be the first. PLEASE level off for a few minutes!"

He just chuckled and replied, "Hey, it's BBQ Day at Lebanon (airport), I think let's sit down for a while and grab a bite." One thing about CH, he knew every airport and what they may be serving for lunch on any given day. I was just glad for a break, and as much as I love BBQ being from the Kansas City area, I made sure to not eat too much as I didn't know what the rest of the day would bring, especially with CH in a playful mood.

I loved flying fire patrol so much that I was asked to help train some of the other agency pilots. See, fire patrol was just a seasonal part of their job. They flew the fleet of planes and helicopters year-round, taking staff and employees all across the state to meetings, conducting waterfowl surveys, deer surveys, you name it, if it had to do with forest, fish, or wildlife and required a plane or helicopter, they flew it. However, it seemed fire detection and size up was not a strong suit for most of them. That is where I came in. I would relay what and why we were doing what we were doing and explain in detail what I was seeing. The big thing was explaining what the ground resources needed from us in the air.

One new to the agency pilot took a bit of time to get trained up. He had lots of hours, but this was definitely new to him. The first couple of times I flew with him when we spotted a fire and needed to circle up to talk to the guys on the ground, he flew higher than normal and in wider circles. I kept trying to explain we needed to get lower and tighter so I could see what I needed to see. He, having never done this before, seemed to hear me but just couldn't manage to get much lower. It took some time, but he eventually became a good fire pilot and could even fly by himself without someone like me in the other seat.

So far, all I have talked about is a fixed wing, but by far, my favorite is when we got to go roter-wing, or as we know them, helicopters. The agency had a Bell Ranger and only got to use that under a few circumstances. First, if all the planes were either busy or down for required maintenance, we got the helicopter, or when we were having lots of larger fires, we would use the helicopter to fly around to each of the fires, land, pick up the Incident Commander and take them for a quick flight around their fire. Once done, we would drop them off and then head to the next fire and pick up that IC. I think this was one of my best memories of flying.

As I couldn't have all the fun, we tried to spread around the flight time to all of our crews. Some took to it and enjoyed it, others did pretty well at it, but some vowed never to get in another small plane again after just one flight. I can't blame them. Flying fire patrol is not for everyone. You are in a small aircraft, flying tight circles over the fires, in and out of the smoke, and usually, a good fire day meant the turbulence was also churning pretty good, especially about early afternoon as the ground really started heating up.

Overall, I helped train up many agency pilots and numerous ground firefighters to be spotters. I had my favorite pilots and favorite aircraft. And, even though I think getting rid of fire towers is a big mistake, I will hold closely the fond memories of flying fire patrol over West Central Missouri as one of my career highlights, and due to my stomach of steel, I never did puke while flying.

Photo from the detection plane where we had a number of arson fires in the area. This shows 3 separate fires all in close proximity.

We called this one in and kept on our mission. By the time we came back around, the crews had this one done and mopped up.

Chapter 22

Last Fire of the Season

Smoke and Mud

In what ended up being the final fire of the 2009 spring season, we had a bit of excitement. We got a call late one evening in April about a fire on NE 75 road, or as we all called it, Hog Lot Road, in St. Clair County. This is an area that the local fire bugs hit about every 3 or so years, and we thought maybe they forgot about it this particular year. The local fire department had been on the scene for a while and were needing some assistance with getting a handle on it.

I knew we had a pretty good chance of heavy rain overnight, and I also knew that where we were headed had very limited cell phone coverage. So, on my way to the fire, I made a quick call to the NWS in Springfield. As it happened, Drew was on duty that evening. Drew was a NWS Senior Meteorologist who also happened to be the Fire Weather Lead. He helped teach S-290 at our Midwest Wildfire Academy and also came out to some of our local fire refreshers every year to discuss the weather. He was very tuned in to what we deal with on the fire lines.

Anyway, I told Drew what we had going on, where we were going to be, and that I needed to know how long we had before the rain hit. Drew informed me that the rain was actually going to be a fairly significant squall line with very heavy rain and gusty winds. He also informed me that the current South winds were going to increase in intensity as the front got closer to us. That was not good news, as we already had a pretty stiff wind as it was. I told Drew that where we were going had very limited cell service, but if I needed any updates, I would try to utilize the Sheriff's Office Dispatch to relay info. We had good radio communication with the Sheriff's Office, and they could make a phone call if needed.

As I arrived on the scene, I met up with the local fire department Incident Commander. He got me up to speed, and together, we worked up a new plan of attack for our combined resources. While the area was somewhat remote, it did have a number of hunting cabins spread out through the area. Some were down trails that looked like they hadn't been used in years. With the fire rapidly advancing, the wind picking up, and the rain and possible severe weather coming, I made the recommendation that we just worry about structure protection. We divided up into groups and started driving down anything that looked like a possible trail or old road. When we came to a cabin, we burned out around the cabin, and once we were certain the cabin was secure, we went on to the next one, and so on.

I don't know if it was pure luck or what, but we seemed to find the cabins with just enough time to get burned out around them before the main fire hit, and then we had just enough time to drive out and be safe. After everyone had done this to about 14 or 15 structures, we were pretty sure we had all the cabins accounted for. I headed back up to the ridge and the main road.

I could see lightning flashing to our NW and knew we were running short on time. Then, my phone rang. Not expecting to have enough signal for a call, it actually scared me enough to jump in my truck seat when it rang. I'm just glad no one was able to see me jump so much, as it would have been a bit embarrassing.

It was Drew from the NWS office, and he was concerned about our safety and rapidly approaching severe weather. Since I had St. Clair County Dispatch pass on a GPS location to Drew earlier, he knew exactly where we were and had been watching the approaching line of storms. He basically told me to get everyone out of the woods and into a vehicle and, if possible, leave the area. We were to expect 70-80 mph winds and quarter-size hail, and we had about 5 minutes before it hit. Thankfully, he got all that info relayed before I dropped the call.

I got on the radio and alerted all fire resources of the immediate severe weather threat and for everyone to disengage. I instructed everyone to call on the radio when they were safe in a vehicle. Just as the last person called in, the gust front hit, and while I don't think we got hit with anything close to 70 mph winds, maybe 45 or 50, almost immediately, we did get the hail and very heavy downpour. I was so glad to be safe and secure in my truck.

Of course, with the rain and the fact that we were on a dirt road that was getting very muddy very quickly, I just ordered everyone out to the pavement about 2 miles away. No one got stuck, and everyone was released from the fire. I drove most of the way home in the downpour but was lucky enough to walk into the house in only a light sprinkle as the squall line had just passed.

The next day, I drove out to see in the daylight what happened the night before. While the road was a bit muddy, there was enough rock to keep from getting stuck. It turns out that we did indeed find every cabin that we needed to; none were lost to the fire. In mapping out the fire, it burned about 450 acres and became one of the more memorable fires I have fought.

It also is a great example of the close relationships we had with our partners, in this particular case, the National Weather Service. Had I not talked with them earlier about our situation and then had I not received the heads-up call, we surely would have been caught outside the safety of our vehicles when the gust front of the storms hit. We were able to keep about two dozen firefighters safe that night.

Sometimes the end can come very abruptly. At least we made it to the roads before the toad choking rain hit.

Chapter 23

Prescribed Fire and Notifications

Who Do You Call

This story is a lesson I learned about who to notify of your intent to conduct a prescribed fire. I am always learning. Learning from my experiences, learning from others' experiences, and just always filling another slide into the carousel.

Mid to late September 2001, the country was still reeling from the attacks of September 11th on the World Trade Center, the Pentagon, and Flight 93. Everyone was on high alert, along with a somber feel in the air. There were still incident management teams who normally managed wildfires, helping manage the recovery efforts at the attack sites. Life still had to keep moving, and there was still work to be done.

We had been working on a natural community restoration project on one of the agency properties, where we had cut all the cedar in an effort to restore a glade. Glades are shallow soiled, rocky side slopes that really can't grow much for trees other than the invasive cedar. They are a great spot for native grasses and forbs. When you remove the cedar and re-introduce fire to the landscape, they respond with wonderful forb and wildflower re-growth.

We were coming into a good weather window, and it looked like everything was coming together to pull the burn off successfully. It was time to start pulling together our crews and making all the notifications that needed to be made. By this time in my career, I was part of a teaching cadre that helped develop an updated fire training curriculum for both wildfire suppression and prescribed burning for our agency. Part of this training was a unit on burn plan development and burn day notifications. We always told students to expect the unexpected. Over plan, get the details.

As this particular project was going to be extremely visible from a major highway and near adjacent sub-divisions, we went about making the notifications. We called the County Dispatch, which usually will make all the other calls for us, like the local fire district and local police. However, we made these additional calls ourselves just to be double safe. This included the local fire district, the city police, the sheriff's office, the state highway department, state patrol, many of the neighboring sub-divisions or homeowners' associations, and local media outlets. The National Weather Service as well due to us requesting spot weather forecasts and wanting updates. For this burn, we also notified our state office. We had everyone covered. Or, so I thought.

We proceed to ignite the burn, and it was progressing slowly, but like we wanted it. Smoke was light and was dispersing great due to the ideal weather conditions. We got to the point where it was time to complete the burn by closing the ignition line and sending a head fire up the hill through the thickest of the fuels. This produced a large black plume of smoke that stood up pretty tall.

Within 5 minutes of this smoke plume going up, I heard a screaming jet engine, looked up, and I swear I was looking eye to eye, or at least eye to visor, of the lead of a pair of A-10 pilots! Holy moly! What happened! It was really obvious they were very interested in our smoke as they turned a number of tight circles and made a number of "runs" over and near us.

See, this was September 26th, only 15 days since the attacks, and everyone, and I mean everyone, was still on high alert. We were only about 35 air miles from Whiteman Air Force Base. I would find out later that these two A-10s were already in the air. I never did know if it was a training mission or a heightened patrol, but when they saw the dark plume of smoke, they made a beeline straight for us. As the story was relayed to me much later, the air base was scrambled, and additional fighter jets were launched. I didn't even think to include the US Military on my list of notifications.

Working so close to Whiteman Air Base, we were used to seeing all manner of military aircraft on almost a daily basis. But this was a first for me to see them so up close and personal. I have been on the air base due to screening excess military property that we would get to help our fire department partners; I had been there working with the local Base Natural Resources lead on tree-related issues near base housing and had met some of the pilots at local career fairs that everyone attended. A while later, at a career fair, I struck up a conversation with a couple of pilots who were in attendance about that day. While I can't confirm anything, the smiles on their faces when I mentioned it gave away enough. They would not confirm any details about that day other than to say they were aware.

Even as I write burn plans these days for projects, I don't know that I have ever put an air base or military installation on the contact list, but it sure crosses my mind every time now. I look a little farther out now as to who may be impacted or how they may be impacted. Who do you call?

The more complex the burn, the more notifications you probably need to make. This is a quick briefing with some Meteorologists form the local National Weather Service office and the local fire department on the tasks for the day. Photo by Tammy Shroyer

Chapter 24

The "Other" Bear Incident

Can you Whisper-Shout?

We were on a fire in Montana, and as was usually the case, our crew was assigned an old school bus to transport us from camp to the fire each day. The bus ride was slow, long, and treacherous as we wound up the mountain, we wondered how we made it around each switchback in the road. From the time we left camp until we got to where the bus would park for the day ended up being about a 2-hour ride. Of course, everyone wanted to stay hydrated and also get an early jump on the hydration meant that 2 hours on a bumpy mountain road in an old school bus was cruel and unusual punishment on our bladders. As soon as the bus stopped at the Drop Point, there was a mad scramble of 20 people out of the bus and to the edges of the clearing to relieve the pent-up bladder pressure.

This became a bit of a routine, and every day, each one of us seemed to go to the same spot to release said bladder buildup. It was also becoming apparent that everyone who came to this drop point was in the same boat. The other crew, dozer bosses, dozer operators, and overhead everyone got into the same routine. Well, after a couple days, we heard there was a bear that was hanging around the drop point. We didn't know if he was displaced by the fire or was looking to score a free lunch as it seemed every firefighter would have something they didn't like in their sack lunch, and even though it is not supposed to happen, food does get thrown out occasionally.

While I and everyone else on my crew had not seen any of the signs, tracks, or scat that others had seen, we just figured it was a matter of time. Anyway, back to the bus ride. I don't know if the bus driver was just out to get us or if the bus was actually getting tired of going up and down the mountain, but the rides up each morning started to get longer and longer. We went from 2 hours to 2 hours and 10 minutes, then to 2 hours and 15 minutes for each ride up. This was killer on our bladders, and some of the crew started resorting to "recycling" Gatorade bottles in the back of the bus.

Well, on one particular day, my bladder was straining and screaming at me pretty bad as we pulled into the clearing at the drop point. I bolted from the bus to hit my normal spot. I ran as best I could with a full bladder, and once positioned, I unzipped my fire pants. It was about this moment that I saw in front of me, not 10 feet away, a bear staring at me. I freeze! He seems intent on just staring, and maybe I startled him into not moving just like he did to me. I tried to whisper-shout to a fellow crew member just a few feet away about my situation, but he did not hear me. I whisper-shout a little louder and prepare to zip up and run if the bear even flinches. Now, keep in mind my bladder is screaming at me at the top of its lungs, and I wonder if the bear can hear a screaming bladder or not. I am not going to find out and implement my plan of self-preservation. In one fluid (no pun intended) motion, I zip up my pants and bolt from my spot. I holler, "Bear!" as I frantically search for another bladder relief spot that has been vacated and with a few fellow crew members between me and the bear. This stirs up a flurry of activity and running and shouting by others close by as they try to figure out where the bear is. At this point, I really don't care, as I was successful in finding an open bladder relief spot and was currently relieving my poor bladder. I just tried to point in the direction of the bear to get folks to leave me alone to finish my business.

At this point, enough eyes had spotted the bear, and they finally noticed that it refused to move, which seemed odd, given the circumstances. Someone threw a rock at it and actually hit it in the head, and it still did not move. Ok, what is going on? This was just not natural.

Turns out, this bear was a full-body taxidermy bear that some of the local dozer operators brought up to scare their dozer boss, who coincidentally used the same bladder relief spot as I did. They had placed it to look like it was standing and leaning out from behind a tree, and it sure did its job with me. Well, since I was the one who allowed the rest of the crew to have a good laugh, I decided I would at least get a picture with the bear. I climbed down to where he was and had a couple photos taken. Once we were all done, we headed out to the fire line for our assignment that day.

Upon returning to the drop point that evening to get a long bus ride back to camp, it was learned that the dozer operators did scare their dozer boss as well, and they got a bonus laugh out of hearing how well it worked on me. Of course, the next day, the bear was gone; they had taken it back with them. But, as I hit my normal spot, my eyes were keenly aware of my surroundings, looking out for a bear or whatever may be looking at me this time. There was nothing this time, and I was able to satisfy my screaming bladder in peace and laugh at myself a bit, thinking back to the day before.

View from the top of the mountain.

Photo of me and the Bear.

Can you see the bear?

Chapter 25

Pagami Creek Fire

15 Days in the Wilderness

After staying fairly busy all summer with our own fires around Missouri, opportunities to get out of state were very limited. We finally got a little relief in the form of rain and calmed things down a bit, but fire season out West was also starting to wind down. There were a handful of large fires in Montana late in the season, but none looked too promising to get called to. Just as I was beginning to think we wouldn't get a detail, I got a call from my Dispatcher. She offered a Crew Boss assignment to Minnesota. To be perfectly honest, I wasn't really looking to take a crew out again, but as this looked like my only opportunity to get a detail, and I knew almost all of the crew members who would be on the crew, I took the job. After getting my copy of the crew resource order, I tried to look up the fire on the Situation Report but could not find it. In fact, there were not even any fires listed for Minnesota. I actually thought there may be a mistake, and we were really going to Montana, as that is where all the fires were. No, Minnesota is where we were ordered to. Ok, but I remembered the last time I was in Minnesota on a fire detail. No fire, not even any smoke, and lots of bridge building.

We all gathered at Rolla at the Mark Twain National Forest Headquarters and, early the next day, took out in a convoy of vehicles. The trip was pretty uneventful, and we rolled into Ely and checked in. We were going to be on a small fire in the Boundary Waters Canoe Area Wilderness. Also, the only resources on the fire were to be our 20-person crew and a 10-person module, in addition to a couple overhead. As with any fire in the Boundary Waters Wilderness, Canoe Safety Training was required. This was a good idea as many firefighters may know how to canoe, but transporting all our gear, tools, food, etc., across many lakes and portages was a different story. Finally, we were ready to launch.

We put in 10 canoes, 2 people per canoe, along with 3-day food barrels, hand tools, chainsaws, fuel, our personal gear and tents, squad tarps, and the kitchen sink. I personally feel that if we had left the kitchen sink behind, we would have maybe had about a full inch of freeboard on the side of the canoes. All told the paddle-in was not too bad, a couple hours and only two portages. The big surprise was that no one swamped their canoe, and all our gear stayed dry. I still wonder to this day how that happened. Being as we were in the wilderness, we still had to follow wilderness rules and could not camp all 20 of us in one campsite. We were given 3 campsites within fairly close proximity, only about a 15-minute paddle from each other. I broke the crew up into three squads, and my Assistant Crew Boss and I each picked a squad to camp with.

The first few days, it was damp and rained a bit. The fire was laid down so much we really could not see it. Our assignment was to make sure the fire did not spread past a handful of critical portages, so we went to work setting up hose lays and sprinklers on the "fire" side of each portage. The idea was to create a rainforest that was so wet the fire would not cross and not reach the portage. This would protect the integrity of the portage. There were 4 portages we were assigned, but 2 were the most critical, so we spent a fair amount of time with those. Now, while we were in designated wilderness, we did have exemptions to utilize chainsaws and pumps to accomplish our work. And even though we didn't fire up a chainsaw the whole time, the pumps were great for what we were doing. We had an unlimited supply of water, of course, and we used it.

The cool thing about this assignment is how we accomplished our tasks. With the instructions to not impact the portages (there was still public out using the lakes) and the fuels pretty thick in the area, we devised a plan to utilize the sprinklers. About 50 yards in from the portage, we crawled through the thick forest and picked out a young tree that would be about 2-3 inches in diameter at about 12 to 15 feet off the ground. I think everyone took turns climbing up a select tree until it started to bend over. We kept going until we were about on the ground with the tree bent over. The top of the tree would be cut off, and the sprinkler with a hose attached would be secured to the top of the tree where it had been cut. Then, very carefully, we would dismount the tree, and it would spring back up carrying the sprinkler with it. This way, when we fired up the pumps, the sprinklers would be about 15 feet in the air and, therefore, get even greater coverage. Once all the sprinklers were in place, the pumps were fired up, and the "rain" began. By spacing appropriately, we were able to get a complete soaking from lake to lake.

With this task completed, our crew was also slated with other jobs. As the weather was warming and drying after the first few rainy days, the fire got more active. A squad was sent to a different part of the fire to assist with mopping up some fire edge. I decided to go along with the squad one day to see that part of the fire and see how they were working. Again, after a lengthy paddle, and crossing a beaver dam on Pagami Creek, we made it to our work area. It was a good mile or two hike along the fire line to where we needed to be so we took off. At this point, one of the crewmembers remembered that he left something in the canoe.

He informed his squad boss and headed back, saying he would catch up immediately. Anyway, I and the squad kept hiking until we got to the area we needed to be. They immediately dove into their task and made quick work of the assignment.

At this point, the Squad Boss notified me that he had not heard from or seen the crewmember who went back to the canoe. With a "missing" crewmember, we started hiking back along the fire line to find him. As we get almost back to the canoes, here he comes up the line, soaked thru with sweat and out of breath. What in the world had happened? Turns out, he was only about 100 yards behind the rest of his squad, but somehow missed the main fire line trail and took instead a section of line that went around a long finger of the fire. Of course, he thinking he should be right behind everyone, he hurries to catch up. The farther he goes, the faster he is going, wondering why he has not caught up yet. Eventually he begins to run trying to catch up. Finally, after a mile or so, he thinks that maybe he took a wrong turn or something and decides to backtrack. At least get back to the canoes and start again. Of course, he is worried about being separated from the rest of the squad and even more worried about what I will say when I find him so he keeps running. He makes it back to the spot where the trail split and he realizes his mistake and starts down the correct fire line. Within a couple hundred yards he runs into us on our way back looking for him. Given the way he looks, soaked thru, dog tired, and out of breath, I give him a chance to explain before I tear into him.

After hearing the story and his efforts to try to catch up and his fear of disappointing not only his squad but me as well, we chalk it up to a very valuable lesson learned. We head back to the canoes and head towards our campsite. While we were all relieved that he was ok, we still did not let him live it down for a while, and his squad put a sign around his neck that evening that said, "My name is _____; if found, please return me to Crew 1."

On a different day, the crew was to assist with some burning, performing ground ignition while the heli-torch performed interior ignition. The crew used drip torches and fusees to light along the edges of the lakes. This was to sort of square things up and keep the fire from making hard runs at our protected portages.

Now, while all these things were going on, "camp" life had some interesting developments as well. Every three days, I would send back a couple canoes to take out our trash, excess supplies, or whatever, and they would bring back the new supply order and a new batch of 3-day food barrels. I selected crewmembers who had strong navigational skills and were quick with a paddle in hand, as it took most of a day to make the round trip and unload and reload supplies. We could not afford to have them get lost or be slow, as our supper that night depended on them.

The other thing we learned was about the food barrels. The first night, there was always some fresh meat, such as steaks, pork chops, or burgers, to cook up. But, by the third night, we were stuck with some freeze-dried something that looked like puke and tasted even worse. On those nights, we started sending a few crewmembers back to camp early with orders to "get a decent supper lined out." This was code for "Go catch a good mess of fish because we are for dang sure not eating another meal of freeze-dried puke in a bag." Again, selecting the right individuals for the job was paramount. As it turned out, it is amazing how good a fillet of smallmouth or walleye tastes when cooked only in butter and salt. It definitely got us through until the fresh meat in the next day's food barrel.

While we are on the subject of food, this detail provided a few more interesting stories as well. Early on, we noticed some chipmunks on our campsite. They were cute and very friendly, eating peanuts and M&M's out of some of the crews' hands. But we would soon learn of their evil plan. Within a matter of days, the 2 or 3 chipmunks grew to about a dozen, and they started to get into everything where food was stored, no matter how secure we thought it was. The numbers seemed to grow to a few dozen as their memos and word-of-mouth communications spread faster than the wildfire we were there to fight.

This was now a huge problem as they were eating or contaminating more food than we could imagine. Something had to be done. Crewmembers put their heads together and came up with a couple ideas to try out. One of the best involved whittling out a pretty hefty slingshot using rubber bands that came in with some of the supplies. After some practice, a couple of the guys got to be deadly accurate. It was about time to wage war. Luckily, the first evening of our battle also coincided with a "day 3" and not much to eat that night. Yes, that is where I am going with this. The guys didn't catch many fish that night due to them being so busy practicing with their slingshots. I will say chipmunk tastes surprisingly sweet, even if it takes quite a few to make a meal. Maybe they were so sweet from eating all our M&M's?

From not much meat to a lot of meat. One evening after shift, some of the guys were exploring a little more of the island we were camped on while others were cooking supper when I heard a commotion down by the edge of the lake. I looked up from what I was doing to see two of the guys bent over at the lake edge and another running towards them. They were yelling and shouting. Then, all of a sudden, the excited shouts turned to groans of disappointment. Seems that one of the guys had snuck up on a beaver and, having grown up like I did, hunting and trapping, knew beaver meat was very flavorful and also would feed us for a couple days. He formulated a plan to lunge and catch it by the tail. That is about as far as the plan went; I think about as fast as he grabbed the beaver's tail, the beaver had a better idea than being our supper and turned to face this unexpected attacker. Of course, the sight of 3-inch teeth that can bite through trees coming at his hands, the firefighter let go, and the beaver slipped into the water safe and sound. He slapped his tail on the water just to express his displeasure with the whole experience. Hearing the tale of what happened as we sat around our campfire eating supper that night, I couldn't help but chuckle a bit, but I have to admit, I was a little disappointed we would not be having beaver roast the next evening for supper.

Getting back to the actual business of fighting the fire, our 2 primary portages were holding fine due to the good sprinkler system we had installed. As the fire progressed deeper into the wilderness, the decision was made to abandon one of our other portages, so we pulled all hoses, pumps, and sprinklers from there. The weather was getting warmer and drier each day, and fire activity was increasing. There were still only our crew and the 10-person module on the fire. We monitored the fire edge as it came around the lake edges and crossed a couple more portages. We would burn out fingers when needed and keep up with maintaining our "rain forest" on the two priority portages. With the fire getting to be a couple thousand acres now and the weather conditions conducive to continued fire growth, the decision was made to start evacuating more public from the wilderness. We had been working with a number of Wilderness Rangers the whole time we were there and had grown fond of all of them. We talked and worked out a plan for who was going to cover which campsites in the new evacuation/closure area.

Over the next 2 days, we didn't work the fire at all and paddled all over, clearing out campsites and assisting people out over the two portages. All told we helped 93 parties out of the wilderness, an unofficial record according to the Wilderness Rangers. The next day, we were to break camp, pack all our gear, and head back to the landing. This was to cap off 15 days in the wilderness, primitive camping, cooking our own meals, and no showers, just an occasional dip in the cold lake to freshen up. Everything was looking good until the weather alert that night. A cold front was coming through the next day, and the winds were expected to be extremely gusty.

The next morning, we didn't fix breakfast and hurried to get all packed up and the canoes loaded. We still had a few hours of paddling to get to the landing, and the winds were coming. We were fine back through the 2 priority portages, but that put us out in a larger lake. The wind was blowing about 40 mph now, and it was going to be a rough go of it. Luckily, the direction we needed to head was with the wind at our back, and then when we needed to cross the wind, we were able to find the lee side of some nicely placed islands. Due to the tough lake conditions, it took a little longer to get back than we had originally planned, but even with loaded-down canoes and wind blowing at times over 50 mph, not one canoe was swamped or lost. A lot of our gear did get wet with the splash of the waves and our paddles, but we made it back nonetheless. During this wind event, all lakes were closed to canoe travel due to the high winds. Of course, the winds on the fire also had a major effect. Once back at Ely and going through the demob process, the plume of smoke was monstrous.

We would find out later that the fire made a major run of about 90,000 acres. Many of our Wilderness Ranger friends we had worked with all week were still out in front of that thing, evacuating the public from the rapidly advancing fire. You can read the report of the Pagami Creek Entrapment from the Wildfire Lessons Learned website if you want, but a number of those Wilderness Rangers had to deploy their fire shelters or take refuge in a lake by intentionally swamping a canoe to escape the fire. I heard later that one of those folks got out of the fire, left the Forest Service, and still is fighting the demons from that day, and I can't blame them. Another has come to terms with the survival and now goes around giving talks on the experience. Of course, with the fire growing so large, firefighters from across the country were called in to help contain the blaze. I heard stories from hotshot crews who got snowed on while working the fire and others who had days of dirty mop-up.

For me, the Pagami Creek Fire will hold a special place in my heart for all the unique things my crew got to do, from truly being camped in the wilderness fending for ourselves to the daily canoe rides to working with such a fine crew of dedicated firefighters. There are so many more stories I could have related to that fire, but maybe later in a different setting.

Here I am briefing to a task that we were just given regarding the assist of public across the critical portages. Photo by Kari Greer

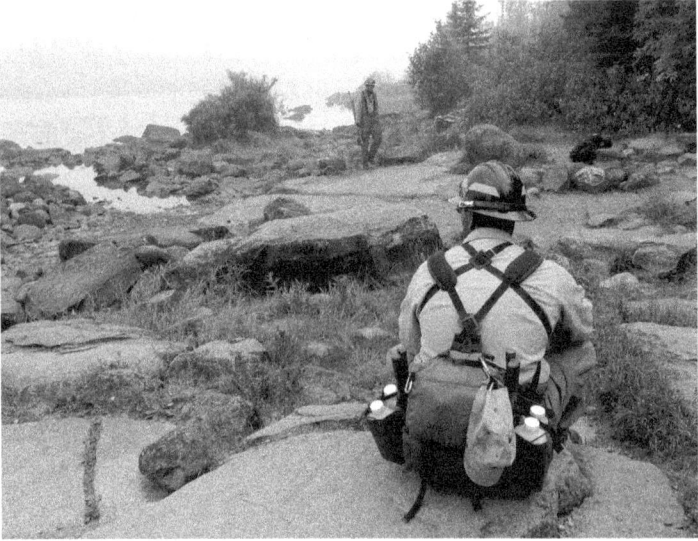

Grabbing a quick break on a nice comfortable rock.
Photo by Kari Greer.

This is the day of the blow-up. We had finally reached the office
and started the check out process and this is the view we had of the
fire as it raced across the landscape.

Yep, we will definitely eat well tonight!

Chapter 26

The Great Boot Debate

Best Foot Forward

What collection of stories about foresters or firefighters would be complete without some comparison of boots? These days, especially with social media, everyone has the ultimate, end-all opinion. I read an innocent question posed by some newcomer on which boots to buy, and honestly, I just go to read the comments. It can actually become quite humorous to see folks get on a rant and then start arguing with each other on what is THE best boot. It is about like asking what is the best truck or what is the best hunting rifle caliber. Everyone is an expert, and everyone is absolute in their likes and dislikes.

With that, I am going to jump on that bandwagon and give you my opinion on the matter. So, what are the absolute best boots to wear? Drumroll, please…. The ones that work for you. Yup, it is that simple. Different people have different feet, and therefore, different boots will do better for them than others. I have actually switched brands over the years. My very first pair of "Forester" boots were Redwings Logger style. These were cheap and served their purpose while I was finishing up forestry school. Cheap being the key word here as spending the money for them was hard enough on our limited budget as newlyweds still in college.

Once I got a full-time gig, I saved up a bit of money so I could get my first pair of Whites in the Smokejumper style. These have been a standard in the profession for quite some time, and most of the older foresters I knew wore these all the time, so it was just a matter of time before I got my very own pair and became one of the cool foresters. Now, I had heard all manner of ways to break in White's. One must wear them for 80 hours straight. Or fill them up with warm water and then put them on and wear them dry. Or soak them overnight in 30-weight oil. Well, I could not bring myself to do some of those outlandish ideas for this expensive pair of boots and just started wearing them every day.

They were slowly getting broken in at the expense of my feet, specifically the notorious "bite" on the top of the ankle. Then, one day, we had heavy, wet snow, and I was scheduled to be in the field, err, forest, all day. It wasn't too cold so I just wore them. After a full day in wet snow, my boots were soaked through. My feet were cold, wet, and sore, but after many miles through the hills doing inventory and the ride home, my boots ended up drying out. I will say that after that, those boots fit perfectly, so maybe there was something to be said about filling them up with water and wearing them dry.

One thing that everyone gets right is to be sure to take care of your boots. If they get dry, oil them. If you think they are getting dry, oil them. If they get dirty, clean them, and I don't mean a little dust; I mean if you wear them through the mud, get the mud off, and then wear them in the woods again to get the rest off and then oil them. Again, good boot care will make the investment in your boots pay off with a long life.

Now, I have had a few pairs of the White's Logger/Smokejumper style boots. Whites, among others, are able to be rebuilt, and I figured that if I had to send in my boots to get rebuilt, what was I going to wear during the 6 to 8 weeks before I got them back? So, I ordered a new pair and got them good and broke in before I sent the other pair in to be rebuilt.

For me, the biggest issue was the soles wearing out too fast. The flint and chert rocks of the western Ozarks in West Central Missouri could chew through just about any boot sole quickly. While early in my career, I pampered my boots by working in the loess hills of the Missouri River bluffs, where you really had to work hard to find many rocks, once I got to Clinton, things changed quickly. In addition to wearing the soles off, I also had some issues with the heels of my boots getting torn up as well, again, due to the rocks I was working in daily. This is really due to the shape of the heel in that it slopes from your heel slightly forward. It makes for better walking, in my opinion, but offers less protection than other types of boots whose heel juts back a ways.

Anyway, I started hearing about people having good luck with Nick's Boots. Apparently, as the story I heard, there were a few folks who had all started working at Whites that went off on their own and started making boots. I don't really know the whole story, and frankly, I don't really care, but Nick, Drew, and Frank, I think, all worked at Whites at some point, and now all have their own boot company. Good for them. And while I didn't make it a goal to meet all of them, I did end up purchasing a pair of Nicks Hotshots. I will have to say that as for the Nicks, they did take a bit, ok, a lot longer, to break in. The leather is a bit heavier. But, once they are broken in, I feel they were a better boot for hiking the mountains.

An interesting observation of mine is that these Nicks kind of feel like my first pair of Whites. I wonder if Whites changed their leather grades over the years, switching to lesser grades. Ask around, and some folks with swear they cheapened up, and others will swear they are the same as before. I don't know for sure; I just have my observations. Anyway, as my son was thinking of getting into my line of work, I told him to get a good pair of boots right off the bat and not skimp with a cheap pair. As I have both Whites and Nicks, the family conversation finally leads to which ones he should get. Well, the Nicks won out, and due to the high cost of the boots, we paid for half of the boots. I mean, Tammy and I bought 1 boot, so what can anyone do with 1 boot? Nate had to buy the other one.

I will say that Nate didn't do anything special; he just wore his boots every day on the mountain, and he was able to break in his boots within 3-4 weeks. It was interesting that after his first summer of wearing those boots every day, he said to me, "I now know what you were talking about." Well, I didn't even know what I was talking about, so I had to ask what he meant. He reminded me that in years past, I would make comments after wearing shoes for a weekend that I just wanted to put my boots back on; they felt so good and comfortable. He was at this point. He was so used to wearing a good pair of broken-in boots that if he went a few days without wearing them, he started craving the "boot feeling" again. Yep, another convert.

I have, in recent years, also started wearing more of a hiking-type fire boot, or Lowa, Baffin Pro, to be specific. It does meet the standard of a fire boot for wildland firefighting. There are just days that it feels good to wear that hiking boot instead. If we are fighting fires in the flat, sagebrush country, these work great, but I did find out they are not for me when in the steep mountain country. Case in point, I was going to help my BLM friends with a prescribed fire on Noon Point. I had my Nicks in the truck with me but was wearing my Lowas. This was a burn in some moderately rough mountain country, and I even told myself I should just change boots really quick. I didn't listen to myself and, later, would regret that decision. After a full, long day of up and down and side sloping while dragging a drip torch, by the time I made it back to my truck that evening, my ankles hurt, and I had worn huge blisters on my big toes. Never would I have ended up with blisters like that if I had my Nicks or even an old pair of Whites on. Oh well, lesson learned.

It all boils down to this, being a forester and a firefighter, your feet are critical. Therefore, your choice of boots is also critical. Wear the ones that work for you. It may cost some money to try and find the right brand and style, but in the long run, it will be well worth it. Some swear by names such as Danner, Drew's, Franks, or Redwings. Younger foresters and firefighters may swear by names such as Lowas, Sportivas, or something similar. But for me, if I need to buy another pair of boots, I might get another pair of Whites, I will probably always keep a pair of Lowas handy, but more than likely, I will get another pair of Nicks, as they are THE only boots anyone should buy. I mean, any other opinion must be flawed, right?

Regardless, I often think about the song called "Boots of the Forester" by the Black Irish Band. They wrote the song in honor of Gifford Pinchot and the USFS. It is a catchy tune, and I highly recommend looking it up and taking a listen. Early on, one of the lines is "… rising with the morning sun, lacing up his boots," and I can tell you that was true so many days in my career. The chorus goes like this,

> *"Oh, the boots of the forester will hike a thousand miles,*
> *up ridges steep, down canyons deep,*
> *through the pristine and the wild…"*

In my mind, this can describe every forester and wildland firefighter I know. I even catch myself singing this in my head as I work. Later in the song, he talks about where the boots hike,

"in the hot coals of a fire,
on a bed of fallen leaves,
the snowy depths of winter,
the flower of buzzing bees."

Again, I have been through it all, as he describes in the song. A wonderful narrative captured for a profession that is not usually sung about.

As I wrap up this great debate, I wanted to include a poem I wrote about my favorite pair of boots. Yes, I still have them. I can't allow myself to get rid of them. They were my first pair of Whites all those years ago. Too many memories and sentimental value. So please enjoy These Old Boots...

Photo of my boots by Tammy Shroyer

Chapter 27

These Old Boots

By Josh Shroyer

These old boots have carried me many miles, over many hills and up many mountains.

They carried me through more fire seasons than I probably should admit.

I drug them through the mud of the Mighty Missouri River, really just a muddy fountain.

I gave them an icy bath in the cold waters of Northern Minnesota. Not a big hit.

They endured all manner of stinging, biting, thorny, prickly things in Arizona,

And wheezed with every step from the volcanic dust of the Pacific Northwest.

From the PJ in Utah and the pine in Montana and California,

Many points in between, No matter the terrain, they always gave me their best.

These old boots have been rebuilt a time or three.

After all these years, I hope not the same for an achy knee.

They are my original pair of fire boots, many the years, you see,

Older than many of the rookies out there, most now in better
shape than me.

Each time I sent them off, to the rebuild shop in Spokane,
I always walked, I never ran,
It was like sending off a friend, you fear you'll never see
I hope the work is good, please come back to me.

And each time they came back,
I excitedly opened the box,
They felt so good as we hit the black,
These old boots, and some good wool socks.

I thought they were retired a few years ago,
But couldn't bring myself to watch them go.
I saved them back with some encouragement from my wife.
She had some idea in her head for them of a different life.

As I sit here today pondering all the memories,
These boots seem to come alive and call out to me,
"Could we share one more hike?
I'll give you one more day, I know you'll like!"

See, they can't be rebuilt any more.
The uppers finally gave up and tore.
And while they will retire to a life of ease,
I figure they are right. One more hike, please?

As I laced them up for our final adventure together,
I couldn't help but wonder about the life of that old leather.
I can tell of the stories grand,
About the fires, and the stands,

162

Of sights we've seen, of trees we cruised,
Of fires put out, us not beaten, but sometimes bruised.

I would be easy on them this round,
An easy hike over level ground.
No smoke, no soot, no hot ash or embers, please.
You've earned your rest, this life of ease.

At other retirement celebrations,
While some may holler and hoot,
As I walk through God's creation,
These are mine. These Old Boots.

Tammy was nice enough to come along and grab some photos of my last hike with my original fire boots. Oh, the miles those have covered. The stories they could tell. Photos by Tammy Shroyer

Photo by Tammy Shroyer

Chapter 28

That's Your Division, Go Catch It

Thrown in the Hot Seat

In early 2015, after a lot of discussion with my better half, I made the decision to make good on my personal goal of moving to Wyoming. I had always said that when I retired, I was going to grab my wife and live a wonderful retirement life in the wilds of Wyoming, but due to a number of circumstances, I was afforded an opportunity to get there a bit sooner.

As I was the "New Guy" again, for the first time in about 25 years, I knew I would have to slowly prove myself to the locals. I mean, what could a firefighter from Missouri really know about fighting fires, right? I moved in the spring of the year, and between the snow and the rain, I wondered if I ever left Missouri. The locals kept telling me this was not normal, but rainstorm after rainstorm, dumping inches of rain, seemed to be the norm for the time being. Having traveled the West enough to know, I was just patient that drier weather was on its way. 2015 in Wyoming went on to become one of the wettest on record, with rain up through late June. Of course, this meant lots of grass growth, and when that finally dries out, it becomes fuel.

As it was, it was late July before I even got on my first fire in Wyoming after moving. It was an 80-acre fire started by a large transmission line being blown down in one of many high-wind events. I ended up getting on it the second day and assisted with some mop-up with one of the County Engines. As the summer went along, I got on a handful of smaller grass and sage fires, but nothing really to speak of. I did make it on a good Type 3 fire outside my District, but that can be another story for another time. Also, to end the 2015 season, later in October, we had a fire go Type 2 in my District, and I got to play Agency Rep again, another story for another time.

Back to late September. I had taken my family to Casper for Nate's birthday dinner and to do a little shopping. On the way back that afternoon, about 50 miles from town, we saw a pretty good column of smoke, and the guessing game began as to where it may be located. It grew, then it went down a bit, then grew again. I knew this would be a fire I would end up on. As we got back into town, I texted Craig, the Fire Warden and let him know I was back in the area. If they needed any help, I was available. He called right back and said yes, come on out; he could use my help. He was headed that way as well to become the Type 3 IC. It was called the South Fork Fire, and it was on the Wind River Indian Reservation, BIA jurisdiction. Of course, the County Fire District has structural protection responsibilities, and this fire was more than the local BIA could handle anyway. He also gave me directions on where to meet up with him and his Deputy Chief, Dan, who currently had the fire command.

As I got closer, I started picking up the radio traffic and heard that most of the structures were accounted for and safe, but the fire had jumped the highway and was getting a good head of steam in fresh fuels. Craig was somewhat delayed in arriving, and I found Dan first. He indicated he was going to transfer to Craig as soon as he got there and to be ready for an assignment. At the wide spot on the highway where I pulled over to talk with

Dan, I got out and finished up getting my gear ready and double-checked a tire that I knew was bad.

The rear passenger side tire had a huge chunk of rubber missing, and I could see belts showing. I had ordered a new set of tires, but they weren't supposed to be in until Monday, and today was Saturday. I was a bit nervous about heading off-road as I didn't know how long that tire would hold up in the rocky conditions where the fire was burning. Anyway, I didn't have much time to think about it as Craig was showing up. I overheard a brief conversation between Craig and Dan where I picked up Dan, stating, "I don't know what Josh's quals are, but I know where I want to send him." With that, the wind grew too loud to pick up what Craig was saying. They took off on a dirt trail to a small hill that overlooked the fire as it raced East. I followed.

At the top of the hill, Craig stopped and got out. That little hill offered a great view of the fire. This would be his Incident Command Post for now. I walked up just as he and Dan finished up their conversation and the transfer of command on the radio. Craig asked if I was ready, and I said I was there to help. With that, he pointed at the smoke column coming up from the head of the fire about 2 miles East of our location and stated, "That's your Division; go catch it!" Without missing a beat, I asked what resources I was going to have and was told all he could spare at the time was 2 Type 6 Engines and a Type 4 Engine.

I grabbed the Engine Bosses and introduced myself really quickly, and we took off toward the fire. As we drove over a series of small 2-track trails and occasionally no trail at all, I was a little concerned about my tire holding up as I drove over sagebrush and rocks. I also had a few moments to think that this was probably the first real test that the guys had to test me out and see what I was made of. Truth be told, I felt a strange comfort level with the assignment as chasing fast-moving fires in Missouri was a lot of what I had done over my career and with a lot fewer resources.

Before I even made it to the active fire, just over 2 miles from the highway and where I left Craig and Dan, Craig had already got a few more Type 6 engines from other Divisions and sent them in my direction. Soon after, a couple water tenders, then more engines. The nature of this fire was very much wind-driven. While very long, it was not very wide, and the flanks had trouble sustaining active fire. Only in lower areas where there was more fuel were there fire concerns, and I knew there were plenty of engines working those flanks. With good black in front of us and resources picking up the spotty active fire edge behind us, I knew we were in a safe place to go ahead and engage the fire.

I quickly sized up the situation in my Division. I basically had two heads running parallel about a quarter mile apart, and the good thing was they were both running straight at a rock face with very little fuel. With this natural break, I figured I just might get lucky. Of course, the fire could still find enough fuel to go up and over the rock; it could creep around either end, or it could just spot, and then we would be chasing it another 5 miles to our next place to make a stand, the next highway.

I gathered my resources and divided them up into 2 Task Forces. Each took a flank and worked toward the rock face, where we could hopefully pinch the fire off. I really didn't worry at the time about the area between the heads, as that was the lowest priority at the moment. Craig kept sending more resources, and I kept putting them to use. We ended up getting a SEAT out of Casper to help, but I knew with the load and return time, I would only have about 2 drops. For the first drop, I had the pilot put in a draw that had a bit of fuel in it and could compromise the rock face holding the Northernmost head, and I needed that slowed down until I could get personnel over to work it. This was also complicated by the fact that the fire had jumped a creek, and we could not get trucks across. I was able to have a couple engine crews get across the river on foot and hike up to the draw where the retardant was dropped. They made good work of the fire there and were able to secure that portion of the fire. Along with the rest of the task force I had on that end, they were able to knock down the fire and started mopping up hot spots and flare-ups.

This left only the right flank to consider. Of course, resources kept being sent to me, which was both good and bad. It was great because I had more horsepower to throw at the fire, but at the same time, we were running out of real estate, and it was starting to get fairly crowded with all the tenders, engines, and pickups. What I really needed was a helicopter with a bucket.

I called back to Command to inquire about the type 3 ship I had heard was ordered. They came back and said it had been canceled, but that was the only info they had. Ouch. That hurt. A handful of buckets would have really knocked out the last of the fire. See, there was a creek with plenty of water in it that the fire had just crossed. The turnaround time would have been next to nothing. In addition, I knew I had one last load from the SEAT coming, but with the water close, it could not drop near the waterway.

About that time, the FMO from the BIA showed up to see how progress was going. We talked briefly, and I gave him my plan for how to use the SEAT. I would attempt to go with a split load, hitting two critical areas and hopefully buying enough time. The whole time, I am still being sent additional engines as they become available from other parts of the fire.

The SEAT is finally about back to the fire and calls on the radio asking for instructions. I explain my plan for a split load. The part on a small section far enough from the creek will secure the flank, and the other part on a small head developed at the base of the rock face. If that head built enough steam, it could jump or spot over the rocks and then off to the races again. The pilot agreed with the plan and flew a dry run over each spot so we could confirm the plan and be sure we were on the same page. With that done, he split his load in two drops. Both hit perfectly. After his second drop along the top of the rock face, a single sage bush flared up beyond the retardant line. The pilot saw it, too, and radioed back that he had a 20-gallon water reserve that he could drop to take care of that. With his next pass, that is exactly what he did.

Watching the SEAT's work was something to behold. I think most, if not all, of those pilots are a bit crazy. However, they had always done an excellent job. With the sun about down at this point, there was no time for a Load and Return, so I released him back to Casper with a hearty thank you for a job well done.

It seemed as though as soon as this radio traffic was done, I was asked by Craig if I needed more resources. He had a number of engines available. I finally had to say no and turn down the offer. This, of course, would bring about a bunch of ribbing later. Anyway, as the sun went down, the wind dropped, and a slight humidity recovery helped us get the final parts of the fire knocked down. With this, we were able to make a plan for a night shift to continue to mop up the fire and for the rest of us to head back.

I finally made it back to the Incident Command Post next to the highway. I was relieved in more ways than one. Specifically, my tire was still intact. I would hopefully make it back to town as the rest of the drive was on pavement. I checked back in with

Craig, and he offered up some pizza that was brought out for all the firefighters. As I ate my pizza, the ribbing started with turning down resources, and at the same time, stories of the firefight started being heard as well.

Overall, I ended up having 22 pieces of equipment assigned to me that day. I managed all this by creating 3 separate task forces. The fire ended up burning almost a thousand acres that day, and was transitioned back to a Type 4 Incident Commander for the night shift and the following day. The BIA would take it from there and continue to mop up and monitor it for the next week. All in all, I, as the "new guy," came through with flying colors and proved myself to the locals. It was nice to pass the test and gain some acceptance.

Photo showing the head fire starting to finger out through the sage brush. As more resources became available, we were able to finally get this caught.

About to get this thing wrapped up.

Chapter 29

Hunkering on the Pedro Mountain Fire

Searching for a Legend

As most of my career was tied to crews, sawyers, and various overhead positions, my time on engines, or at least Type 6 or larger engines, was rather limited. So, when a large fire broke out in Wyoming that was going to be run as a Type 3 incident with a State Type 3 team, I jumped at the offer to take one of our agency Type 3 Engines out as the Engine Boss. This fire was in the neighboring district, just a couple hours away, and burning in the San Pedro Mountains. This was the first year the Agency had the Type 3 Engines, and I was excited to help run them through the ringer or, I mean, utilize them.

This was a fairly simple assignment. Lots of acreage was going to burn as the terrain was extremely rough, steep, and rather inaccessible. The overall plan was for the fire to come out of the rough terrain, and we would catch it in the finer grassy fuels on easier slopes. Over most of the almost 2 weeks we were there, we made it around most of the fire perimeter, performing typical engine crew tasks like holding while fire lines were burned out, mopping up, protecting structures (houses and cabins), conducting burn-outs ourselves, and hunkering.

175

What is hunkering, you ask? Well, as on many assignments, there comes a time when you have worked yourself out of things to do, but you are not released yet. This just so happened to us. We were on the southern edge of the fire and had spent a couple days conducting burn-out operations and then mopping up that burn-out. Eventually, even the cold trailing was done. As this was later in the season and there were no other fires going on at the time, the team decided they would keep us on throughout the holiday weekend of Labor Day. You know, just in case.

There was nothing to do for a day or so, but we had to stay gainfully employed. We continued to mop up a few more chains in, code for we were not to be found. It was on one of these days I decided to go for a scouting mission. I just had to gain some better situational awareness.

It is probably at this point I should give some background and history of the Pedro Mountains. In the early 1930s, a couple of miners found a small mummy in a sealed cave that they blew open while looking for gold. What would become known as the Pedro Mountain Mummy, or Pedro, would go in stories and legend and all manner of intrigue. Initially thought of as a fake, it was indeed a real thing. It was extensively tested and proved real, although it was subsequently lost, never to be found again. There are many stories and theories surrounding Pedro. Was this a mummy from the "Little People" from Native American lore? Was it just a small child that died soon after birth? How did it come to be mummified? Was it cursed? Or, maybe it brought on a curse after being found. I guess we will never know at this point. Unless. Unless another is found?

Now, having heard of this legend and knowing we were in the very mountains where this happened, I was intrigued. It would be very interesting if, somehow, I could find the cave where Pedro was found. What if I found another? Was there more out there?

So, on this particular day, after the rest of the crew had established LCES, you know, Locate Cooler, Establish Shade, I told them I was going to check out a good lookout spot up on the side of the mountain. I showed them on the map where I was heading and about how long I planned for my scouting mission. I took off heading for the over yonder and across a couple hollers.

For a place that was usually very windy, I do remember the day being deathly still and quiet. I climbed the slopes, explored every rock, and scouted every hidden crack. There was an intense feeling of being alone. Now, I'm not one to worry about being alone. Remember, I became a master of that while growing up on those dark night trap lines all those years ago. I tried to listen to what little wind there was or hear if the eagles would talk to me and direct my path.

Many hours and quite a few miles later, I hadn't found much on the burned landscape other than a somewhat mummified mountain lion carcass. It appeared to have died of natural causes in a shallow cave and, due to the dry environment, dried out as much as it decayed. While not the mummy I was looking for, I guess it was the journey and not the destination that day. A journey of self-discovery and internal dialog. What did I believe about Pedro? Was it really possible to listen to the wind or hear the eagles speak? Did I have some long-forgotten ancestor walking with me that day that steered me clear of finding something I really didn't need to find? Was the dead mountain lion a warning sign?

I may never know the answers to any of these questions. But as I headed back to the engine and the rest of my crew, the wind picked up a bit, and the world grew back to its normal volume. I could hear a helicopter flying buckets on the other side of the fire and hear the rumbling of a different engine as they moved hunkering spots. I thought back to some other legends I have sought after before, like Sasquatch, probably watching us firefighters while working a fire near Happy Camp in Northern California. Or maybe, as I spent so much of my life in the backwoods of Missouri, always on the lookout for the ever-elusive Karkhagne. As with so many of the legends across the country, this one chose to remain hidden on this day.

I took this photo of a crew member from my engine while we secured a line from a burn out. It got a bit hot in there and he was just trying to keep the green side from igniting. We were successful in holding this section of line on the North side of the fire.

A crew member grabbed my phone to take this photo of me while we were watching a burn out on the South side of the fire.

Chapter 30

Nate's First Fire

Officially, Anyway

This story will capture the series of events of Nate's first official fire as a member of a Forest Service Fuels Crew. However, to say that this was his first fire needs a little explaining. We often joke that Nate's real first fire was in utero, as my wife was pregnant with Nate but was coming out to help on some of the many fires we were having at the time.

Nate learned the jargon and tactics of fighting fires early on just by sitting at the dinner table and listening to two firefighters. He even had a drip torch placed in his hands at the age of 12, as he helped on a prescribed fire on his grandpa's property while we were doing some glade and savanna natural community restoration. He was able to run the leaf blower and handle the radio as well by this time. Over time, he helped on many such prescribed fires as we helped friends and neighbors with their burning projects on CRP, prairies, and woodland burns.

All told Nate had a lot of experience when he finally got hired on with a Forest Service Fuels Crew once he turned 18 and graduated high school. As he was on the fuels crew, they did not make it to help on fire until late July that year when they were called to help with the Brokenback Fire on BLM land. This also happened to be in my district and was an area I knew pretty well as we had not only state land in the area but had been on a few fires in the area as well.

I always figured I would try to get on Nate's first fire, and here was the opportunity. I called up the IC of the fire, a BLM Engine Captain I knew, and asked if I could come out. I explained this was Nate's first fire, and he was excited to have this happen and invited me out. After a couple hours' drive, I was getting close to the area.

On most fires, radio traffic uses the title of the position so that you don't have to remember names. This would be like "Bro-kenback IC, Division Bravo, on Tac 3," "Division Bravo, Bro-kenback IC, go ahead," and so forth. However, I wasn't actually assigned to the fire and was acting more of an Agency Rep as there was state land threatened by the fire. In this case, I used my name when calling. "Brokenback IC, Shroyer, on Command." "Shroyer, Brokenback IC, go ahead." "Brokenback IC, Shoyer, where can I meet up for a face-to-face?"

As most crews on the fire only have some of the overhead, like the crew boss or engine captain listening to the command chan-nel, there was a little confusion among Nate's crew as to what was going on. Looks start getting thrown in Nate's direction, and if I got the story correct, a Squad Boss even came and asked Nate why he was on the radio and especially talking to the IC? Poor Nate. He swore he was not on the radio. He didn't even have a radio.

Of course, in short order, I met up with the IC, and we had a good laugh at what was transpiring and a story of others whose dads had met them on their first fires. They pointed out where the crew was, and I headed down the line to find them. I see Nate before he sees me, and I can't be sure, but I think he shook his head a bit when he finally saw me hiking down the fire line. I don't know all of what was going on in his head, as this is my version of the story. You may just have to get his version someday if he ever decides to write his own book.

Anyway, a short break later, a couple photos, and meeting some of his crewmates, and they were back to work. I hung around for a few minutes and took a few more photos, and then I was off down the fire line to see how close the fire was to our state land section. I mean, that was the whole reason I was here, right?

I'm sure there was some good-natured ribbing at his expense late that night as they ate supper, but also some stories from some of his crew about similar things they had experienced. So many firefighters in the area came from fire families, after all.

Regardless, I was just a proud dad at that moment, being able to share in a "first" with my son as he started his fire career. Officially, at least. And I have the photos to prove it.

While this is not the first photo I grabbed of Nate as I walked up, this is a better one as we had time to pose the shot and he was grinning from ear to ear by this point.

Photo of some "unofficial" fire experience earlier in Nate's life.
He looks like a natural though.

Before leaving Nate and heading down the fireline, I grabbed
this selfie. Just couldn't pass up the chance.

Who knows? Maybe this was Nate's actual first fire.

Chapter 31

What Does It All Mean

It's About People

As I looked back on all these stories, I realized something. There was a common theme in each, whether directly or indirectly. That common theme? People. People are what makes this work. The friends we find along the way, the relationships we build, the connections we make. Even the stories that were of me when I was alone, like the Cat Tracks story, only come alive once I decide to share it with others, to see the humor in it all and use that to create a smile on someone's face. I could have kept it to myself and not shared that embarrassment, but where is the fun in that?

Everything so far has been on the lighter side, and I will keep it mostly that here. However, I do want to say that some of these wonderful people who have come across my path were placed there with a purpose, maybe even divine intervention. A good friend of mine, Terry, has stated that there are no coincidences, only guided steps on this path of life. Unfortunately, the nature of this job has provided way too many instances of loss, death, and destruction. If we kept that all in, we would self-destruct. We must have some outlet.

That is where I feel so many of these people fit in. While we may share and talk about the bad with each other, we also celebrate and revel in the good, sometimes even in the same conversation. We laugh with each other, we share fond memories and awesome sights seen, we remember those who went before us, and we throw a hand on a shoulder when the dust gets in our eyes. That dang blasted dust in the eyes!

Yes, I do believe that everyone on our path has a purpose. Sometimes, I think that purpose is to show us what not to do or what not to say. Sometimes, they are meant to teach us a lesson. Now, that lesson may be how to exercise patience or how to hold your tongue, but a lesson nonetheless. But I firmly believe that most are on our path to share the human experience with us and help us along the way. A shared companionship.

I cherish so many people who have come across my path and have so many fond memories. It doesn't really matter what we are discussing. Sometimes, it is the setting or the circumstances that brought us together, or even after many years, how we reconnected. The conversations have covered politics (always fun!), policies, tactics, family, grandparents, mentors, successes, frustrations, injuries, bosses, employees, employers, agencies, and even the kitchen sink.

As I stated at the beginning, laugh at life, laugh at yourself. Treat others the way you want to be treated. Be the bigger person, but don't allow yourself to get walked over, either. Smile often and share that smile with others. Hold the door for a stranger. Lend a comforting ear without judgment. Love everyone, but especially love yourself. Take care of yourself so that you can take care of your neighbor.

Who would have thought that this small-town boy from Missouri would be here, at this moment, with this story to tell? Who could have counted the number of wonderful people that would be encountered along the way? How can it be that so many things seem to conspire against us, yet the connections are made? I'm happy to be able to share my stories and show you.

Show Me a Firefighter.

Photo of me and Kari, a wonderful photographer, and a great friend. A couple chance encounters on some random fires a thousand miles and a decade apart. One of many cherished individuals who have crossed my path.

As an Operations Section Chief, I was giving a follow-up
briefing to the Public Information Officers assigned to the fire.
Photo by Kari Greer

Kari said to strike a pose and this is the best I could muster.
Photo by Kari Greer.,

Early morning after briefing.
Photo by Kari Greer

This fire had a number of challenges, but being able to have some
hard discussions with someone who I call a close friend made this one
of the more memorable fires. Kristen Honig, another great photographer
on contract from NIFC, was able to capture so much with this
photo me Craig and I. Photo by Kristen Honig

Photo by Kristen Honig

: I saw this snag and had to go get a photo for myself. Kristen snapped this
photo while I was capturing my photo from my phone.
Photo by Kristen Honig.

My photo of the snag.

My friend and one of my mentors, Tim Stanton, gives a briefing before one of the training burns we worked on together. I had invited Tim up to not only utilize his vast experience, but also just an excuse to work with him again. Check out Tim's Book Redwings Through the Forest.

191

Cutting a burning snag on the Tripod Fire in Washington.

FlamingTree
Solutions

https://flamingtreesolutions.com/

www.ingramcontent.com/pod-product-compliance
Lightning Source LLC
Chambersburg PA
CBHW022052020426
42335CB00012B/651